The Big Book of Direct Sales Careers

The Big Book of Direct Sales Careers

www.bigbookofdirectsales.com

Compiled by Michelle McGarry

iUniverse, Inc.
New York Lincoln Shanghai

The Big Book of Direct Sales Careers
www.bigbookofdirectsales.com

iUniverse, Inc.

For information address:
iUniverse, Inc.
2021 Pine Lake Road, Suite 100
Lincoln, NE 68512
www.iuniverse.com

The content in this book is resource information only. Do not enter into any business opportunity without doing your own investigation and obtaining the proper legal advice.
Information herein about individual companies and business opportunities is based on company sales material and is subject to change.

ISBN: 0-595-32570-X

Printed in the United States of America

Contents

Introduction

Direct Selling: The American Dream

As I've written many times before, I love home business. I'm excited about all things entrepreneurial. But I must admit, I was a bit jaded on the subject of direct selling, until I went to a WAHMFest last fall. I was promoting my last book, *Train at Home to Work at Home* and went to the trade show in Virginia where I hosted a booth to promote and talk about my book. WAHMFest (www.wahmfest.org) is a terrific organization founded by Marybeth Henry, a Senior Sales Director with Mary Kay Cosmetics. Its purpose? To help work-at-home moms (like myself) set up work-at-home trade shows for other moms seeking home business opportunities.

I wasn't quite sure what to expect at WAHMFest, and I must admit, when I saw that most of the other booths were direct selling reps, I was disappointed—at first. I mean, when you've researched home business as much as I have, direct selling companies seem to saturate the market a bit—they all start to sound the same. How do you tell one company from the other? But then as I sat there, and occasionally walked around to check out the competition, I was quietly impressed with the whole thing. The products were wonderful—not just Tupperware and Avon we've all heard of, but also new companies and innovative products with fantastic displays that really caught my attention. I was also impressed with the overall professionalism and enthusiasm of the reps themselves, and that most of them genuinely loved the products they sold and seemed to make a good living selling them.

I was impressed enough to write a book about them, not as an analysis of the companies, but as an informational guide for anyone interested in direct selling as an at-home career. It occurred to me that perhaps resistance to beginning a direct selling career began with a misunderstanding of the plethora and variety of companies out there. I now believe that the first step in being successful with direct selling is to choose *the right company and the right product for you.* Every one of these companies promises the following benefits: working at home, more family time, unlimited income, and incentives. But to be really successful, you need to find a product—and a company—you really love.

When I got home, I began some initial research and discovered that there were a wealth of companies out there, both old and new, that needed to be organized in some way, and wouldn't it be nice to put all of them into a book? I realized that direct selling companies have become an integral part of our economy, and I now feel that they are a true extension of the American dream. They exemplify this in its truest sense because most of these companies were started by a single entrepreneur who set out on her own and made a success not only for herself, but also for others like her. The opportunity to start making money right away and be your own boss is the essence of the American Dream.

Direct-Selling Glossary

Downline: The people you recruit into the company. Often commissions are offered on your downline.

Upline: The people directly above you in the company, including your sponsor who recruited you, and her sponsor, etc.

Override: A term referring to commissions received from downlines. An override commission is a downline commission.

Generation: Refers to downline recruits. First generation recruits are those you recruit yourself; second generation are consultants recruited by your first generation, and so on.

Consultant Level: Most companies have opportunities for advancement, including advancement to management levels, often including a title change. Sometimes commissions or quotas change based on your "consultant level" or management level attained.

Let's Give Credit Where Credit is Due

When we're talking about direct selling companies, let's remember something important: Companies like Avon, Tupperware, and Mary Kay were among the very first ever to offer *women* that first step into entrepreneurship and independence. And they're still going strong, changing their products to meet the times, and are among the giants of household names today. Direct selling companies continue in their legacy of offering low-cost startup home businesses to not only women, but everyone, with men quickly growing among the ranks of direct sellers.

The range of companies and products out there is so wide and ever-growing, there is something out there for practically everyone.

And let's talk about incentives and benefits. Direct selling companies are some of the most forward-thinking companies around with their track records of recognition and rewards for successful consultants—rallies, conventions, company car programs, cash and trip incentives—do you know of regular corporate America companies who do this for their employees? Direct selling companies are on the right track as far as reward and recognition. With most companies, new consultants get a designated sponsor to help guide them to success, instead of a boss on their back. Can you imagine your boss sending you to work at home, whenever you wanted, and then give you a trip to Hawaii when you exceeded your sales quota?

Another unique quality to these companies is that most of them are founded on the tenets of family values; they spend a great deal of time on philanthropic endeavors, giving back to the community, and instilling and upholding these values in their consultants.

That said, selling is selling, and if you hate it, direct selling isn't going to be for you. But to be fair, no matter what entrepreneurial venture you take up, selling will always be a part of it. Marketing, promotion, and sales are ultimately the hallmark of any business, whether you're selling a product, a service, or a skill. The trick to *direct* selling is to decide if you will enjoy selling a product, and then figure out which product you can't live without.

My advice has always been this: Find something you love, whether it be a product, a service, an ideal—something that you can get behind 100%. That's what this book is for—to see if there is a product or company that you can fall in love with and build a home business on. In the course of researching these companies, I found a large number of companies that I had never heard of, but was equally surprised and impressed with their products, not only as a business opportunity, but also as new products to add to my shopping lists. This book is meant to provide you with the overview of the companies out there, what each offers you for commissions, and how much it costs to get started.

Breaking Two "Golden Rules" of Home Business?

1. *Never give anyone money to start a home business.*

Direct selling companies are virtually the only exception to the rule: Never pay someone to begin your home business. (The other is franchises.) You'll find that almost no direct selling company allows you to become a consultant for their company for free. You usually have to buy their starter kit, which typically includes sample products and training materials. This is *very* different from home business scams—if you've ever given money to someone who promised to help you make money stuffing envelopes, that's a scam. In order to tell the difference, you need to do your research. Does the company have a physical base of operations or just a P.O. Box? (This in itself is not a general indicator, however. Tupperware, one of the most famous and reputable companies has a P.O. Box.) How vague are the claims they make? Have you ever heard of them before? Do they sell a real product, or just an opportunity? Even with companies in this book, you need to do your research. (During the writing of this book I saw a *Dateline* special about one of the companies I planned on writing about, and had to delete the company based on that special.)

2. *Home businesses are never easy to start.*

As I have written in previous books, it's easy to get caught up in the promises of "Start Today, Earn Tomorrow," promotions, which are rarely true of home business ventures. For their credit, direct selling companies are generally inexpensive and "easy" to start. Because the company's success depends upon the success of its consultants, they want to help you schedule your home parties and sell products. These companies make it as easy and carefree as possible to get the basic materials, training, and support to get you on your way. So having your first home party may be easy to put together; but following this "Golden Rule," sustaining your business is up to you!

34 million people worldwide are engaged in direct selling, an $82 billion industry.

It's Not Just Tupperware and Avon Anymore

What are the hottest trends today in direct selling? Jewelry is hot, especially charm jewelry. Then there's scrapbooking, which is emerging as one of the fastest growing cottage industries in the new millennium and direct selling companies are following suit with scrapbooking and rubber-stamping companies popping up every day. And what are the common themes? The companies that are emerging are focusing on the sentimental, on preserving family memories, and nostalgia for family life. Think about what Author and Futurist Faith Popcorn predicted would be successful in the 21st century in her famous trends: products that make life easier for our fast paced lives (easy-to-make gourmet foods); selling to women as they drive the dollars spent in this economy (almost all the products here); and small indulgences (products like charm jewelry and spa products that make us feel good but don't cost too much). And the success and abundance of candle companies may suggest that we all need a little more fragrance in our lives.

Do Your Homework

Just because a company is described in this book is no guarantee of anything: Always do your own research. I compiled this information because these companies fascinate me and I think most of them have great products that are worth looking into. That said, I can't make a guarantee that any of these companies will help you start your own business. Everyone is different, and you need to find your comfort level and the right company for you. Since I haven't tried out all the companies in this book, I don't know for sure whether you earn 50% commission or if it's really 20% on most of the products. I can only report what the company offers in its official sales material. The rule of thumb is: If it sounds too good to be true, it probably is, or at least merits some additional investigation.

Direct Sales vs. Multi Level vs. Pyramid Schemes

I must explain is the difference between direct sales companies, multi-level companies, and pyramid schemes (which are illegal). Direct sales companies sell products through network marketing—a process by which you get new customers by networking through your current customers. These companies generally offer you commissions on your sales, and may or may not offer you a piece of the commissions from sales reps you bring into the company (downline commissions). But this is not true of all companies. All the companies in this book are direct sales companies. A subset of that group are the multi-level marketing (MLM) companies, who do offer downline commissions as part of your earning potential. Companies that are not multi-level often offer other incentives for recruiting new consultants, including free products or straight cash bonuses. Other companies have no recruitment incentives.

For multi-level marketing companies, there can be a wide range of commissions available. Some companies have a limited number of recruits that they will pay out on (first generation, second generation, etc.) And some companies have multi-level downline commission structures so complex they are too complicated to get into in this book. But just keep in mind that if downline commission is a big deciding point for you, once you decide on a few companies you like, really investigate their downline commissions. In this book you will see a range provided—see below at "Interpreting the Data."

Pyramid schemes, on the other hand, are illegal, and *to my knowledge* (although the information in this book is not guaranteed at all), none of these companies in this book violate the law. Pyramid schemes are based on selling *opportunities* to others, and making money on their recruits selling the same opportunities. A fictitious product may be involved. When in doubt, go the Direct Selling Association and ask them—they are a good resource (www.dsa.org).

You're an Independent Contractor, not an Employee

One of the most important things to remember about *all* of the companies in this book: They are not offering you employment. They are offering you a business opportunity, and as their representative, you are an independent contractor, with tax responsibilities. This has its pluses and minuses. For one, you truly are in business for yourself, so there is a lot of freedom that goes with that. On the other hand, you are now responsible for all the benefits that you would typically receive from an employer, such as health and life insurance, for example. Of course, if this is just a part-time venture for you, this won't be as big an issue.

When Choosing a Company: Ground Floor or Established?

When deciding among the many factors of each company, you may wonder whether it's better to go with a brand new company that promises a "ground floor opportunity," or with one that is established and has a household name. I suggest that there are benefits to both.

An established company obviously offers you the security that it probably won't be going belly-up in a couple of months, as proved by the test of time. There is also the benefit of some companies having well-known products and a built-in customer base, and even in some cases national advertising (Avon advertises new products on television, a plus for their consultants). The downside is that larger companies that have millions of consultants may be saturating the market a bit, and it could be more difficult to get started with customers.

The bonus of a brand-new company is its uniqueness, and some new companies have branched way out of the standard cosmetic and houseware products categories, which makes selling to friends and family (at least to start) a little easier. (Check out some of the gourmet food companies, jewelry companies, and even some of the natural cosmetic companies with fantastic new products.) The other benefit to a new company is the moneymaking potential of being one of their first consultants. If you look 5 years ahead, how many team members will you have if you stick with this company? If the company only has 100 consultants now, and in 5 years has 20,000, you have the opportunity to get in on a large number of those recruits easier than if the company had started at 20,000. The earning potential is staggering. But there is also greater risk with a new company as well. There's no guarantee that a company will be around in 5 years, for one. And you may waste time getting invested in a company that could go belly-up. (Even in the span of time while I wrote this book, two companies went bankrupt and had to be deleted before publication!)

Check out the Quick Comparison Chart on page 159 to compare companies by commissions and starter kit prices.

Interpreting the Data

Why do I provide a range of commissions and starter kit prices? Some companies offer a straight commission on sales while others offer different commissions based on how much volume you sell in a month. Some companies have complicated downline structures (much too complex so for this book to go into) and others have none at all. Then, many companies have different starter kits to choose from, and some you can specify which products you want included, and therefore the price may vary. Or, sometimes there are specials offered on kits; so the range price may be the occasionally available sale price up to the regular kit price. Where it was simple enough to include it, I did specify some downline commissions.

For some companies, you have to have a certain number of active recruits and also sell a minimum per month to receive overrides. Also, every company has their own policy on how many levels you can earn commissions on—some companies have no levels at all, but give you product credit for your recruits. Others have only 1st generation recruit bonuses up to giant multi-level earning potential (up to infinite levels). The purpose of this book is not to give you a detailed version of each company's downline structure, but to give you the *flavor* of each company—their products and purpose, plus an overview of earning potential, so you can narrow the list of companies that could work for you, and then allow you to contact those companies to make an informed decision.

Use this Book as a Starting Place

My suggestion is this: Use this book as a resource and a starting place. Browse first. Open your mind to the new products and companies out there. Then make a list of 20 or so companies that interest you. Try the products. Find some products you really love and would want to share with friends, even if you weren't a rep. Then get in touch the company, who will put you in touch with a rep in your area (or check out if your company is profiled on p. 45). Here are some of the questions to get the ball rolling:

- How long has your company been in business?
- Approximately how many consultants does your company have worldwide?
- How much does your starter kit cost?
- What does the basic starter kit contain, and what is its retail value?
- What is your main sales method? (Home parties, direct selling, online, etc.)
- What kinds of training does your company provide?
- How much support will I receive from my sponsor?
- Do consultants have access to their own online shop/company-affiliated Web site?
- What percent commission do consultants earn?
- What percent commission to consultants earn on recruits?
- Do consultants have to maintain inventory?
- Do consultants have specific territories?
- Do I need to sell a certain amount each month to a) remain active and b) receive override commissions?
- What kinds of incentive and bonuses can consultants earn?
- Is your company a member of the Direct Selling Association (DSA)?
- What are your average sales per party/demonstration?
- How long is an average home party?
- What hostess benefits do you offer?
- If I move, what parts of my business may move with me (team members, customers, etc.)?

A Last Note: Ignore the!!?? Exclamation Points!!

In an effort to be enthusiastic and sell you an opportunity, most of these companies use an excessive amount of exclamation points (a serious obstacle when you're trying to decipher some of this info for a book!, oh sorry, another point). Don't let the enthusiasm with which they explain their company get in the way of your enthusiasm for reading about their products and services.

(Companies marked with a ** are profiled, starting on p. 45)

Affordable Luxuries**

Affordable Luxuries, 569 High Street, Westwood, MA 02090. Tel: 781-326-6800. Fax: 617-663-6007. E-mail: info@affordableluxuries.us. Web: www.affordableluxuries.us.

Affordable Luxuries specializes in scented candles. They craft their own collection of candles in a small chandlery in rural Massachusetts, using a premium soft jelly/paraffin wax blend. The candles come in travel tins or votives, or in their exclusive AL Jars, durable curved-glass vases. They also offer Yankee Candles and root candles (soy). AL's Business Starter Kit costs $25 and provides more than $85 in educational materials, sales tools, and a supply of catalogs. Also included is an AL myWebStore subscription. AL's Home Demonstration Kit costs $199. The Home Demonstration Kit is worth more than $400 and contains all the materials to hold a full-featured "Candle Experience" (their home show and demonstration). The Home Demonstration Kit includes a wide assortment of AL candle and accessory products, educational materials, sales tools, a supply of catalogs, as well as the AL myWebStore subscription. Consultants earn 25–40% commission on sales with 6% on team members, plus 5–8% monthly sales bonuses.

Alabaster Candles at Home

Alabaster Candles at Home, P.O. Box 156, 24744 U.S. Highway 31, Jemison, AL 35085. Tel: 877-621-2325 or 205-688-5222. Fax: 205-688-5225. E-mail: info@alabastercandlesathome.com. Web: www.alabastercandlesathome.com.

Alabaster Candles at Home is a direct-selling candle company based in Alabama. Distributors purchase a distributor kit, which contains a sampling of all their products, as well as selling tools. The cost of this kit is $295. Distributors are encouraged to maintain inventories. They offer two types of candles: container (soy wax) and pillar (paraffin wax). They also offer a new line of bath and body products. Consultants earn 40–55% commission with a $50 bonus for recruits including a 10% commission on first list recruit sales and 5% commission on second line recruit sales.

Aloette Cosmetics, Inc.

Aloette Cosmetics, Inc., 4900 Highlands Parkway, Smyrna, GA. Tel: 1-800-256-3883. E-mail: careeropp@aloette.com. Web: www.aloette.com.

Established in 1978, Aloette Cosmetics, Inc. International Headquarters is based in Atlanta, Georgia. Owned by veteran Atlanta Aloette franchisees, Christie and Bob Cohen, Aloette has grown into one of the country's leading direct sales skin care and cosmetics companies. The Aloette Sales Kit contains more than $800 worth of product, and distributors earn up to 16% management overrides monthly, plus up to 51% on personal sales. Incentives include trips, cars, and prizes. The company offers franchises to those seeking an independent income. Under the current franchise model, franchisees have access to Aloette Cosmetics' Centralized Services Operation. This means all product shipping is done through a central office and franchisees are not required to purchase, store or maintain inventory. The initial term of the franchise agreement is five (5) years, after which the agreement may be renewed in five-year increments. Franchisees must attend and successfully complete a training program provided by Aloette, which is designed to assist with learning of the Aloette system and to sharpen sales and marketing skills. The cost of the training is included in the initial franchise fee of $5,000. Franchisees are responsible for all travel and lodging expenses. You may sell your Aloette Franchise.

The Angel Company™

The Angel Company, 405 Saturn Avenue, Salina, KS 67401. Tel: 785-820-9181. Fax: 785-827-5101. E-mail: tac@theangelcompany.net.
Web: www.theangelcompany.net.

The Angel Company ™ (TAC™) is a multi-level, direct sales company founded in 1997. The company specializes in rubber-stamping products and accessories. TAC™ Demonstrators receive 25% commission on personal net sales, plus override commission on downline sales. Demonstrators also receive a 30% discount on personal orders and 40% off stamp demonstrator discount coupons. The company also encourages their demonstrators to generate additional income by selling their own hand stamped creations. Demonstrators have the opportunity to earn prizes, enter contests, and have their hand-stamped samples featured in their publications.

Three starter kits are available, ranging in price from $75–$300. The $75 Paperwork Only Kit contains catalogs, order forms, and invitations, plus the Demonstrator Manual, recruitment packets, and The Angel Company™ Logo Stamp. The $150 Seasoned Stamper Kit contains the same paperwork, a TAC black stamp pad, Impress Dual Markers, emboss stamp pad, gold embossing powder, and acrylic mount set, plus your choice of unmounted TAC-coded images, up to $125 worth. The Successful Start Kit contains the paperwork, $240 worth of unmounted stamps (your choice), and a larger assortment of accessories (deckle shears, stamp cleaner, marvy heat tool, watercolor pencils, corner punch, paper corrugator, and more) for $300.

Arbonne International**

Arbonne International, Inc., 4 Cromwell, Irvine, CA 92618. Tel: 949-770-2610 or 800-272-6663. Fax: (949) 837-8415. E-mail: customerservice@arbonne.com. Web: www.arbonne.com.

Arbonne International sells skin care products based on botanical principles, and became a reality in the United States in 1980. Arbonne's product line has since grown to include both inner and outer health and beauty products. Independent Consultants earn 35% commission, plus 4% overrides on team members. Consultants also earn $50 cash bonuses on new recruits. The company offers a Mercedes-Benz car program. Arbonne offers the choice of two Starter Kits, the Quick Start Kit for $29 and the Super Start for $65. The company also has a fax-on-demand system from which you can automatically receive the consultant agreement (call 949-455-1004 and request document #520).

AtHome America**

AtHome America, Inc., 5625 West 115th Street, Alsip, IL 60803. Tel: 800-928-4663. Fax: 708-597-1435. Web: www.athome.com.

At Home America specializes home décor, housewares, baskets, bedding, furniture, dinnerware, and candles. Co-founders and sisters Lisa Brandau and Becky Wright, who still handpick each product they sell, founded the company in 1982. Their HomeStyle Specialists earn up to 20–30% commission (depending on volume) and receive discounts up to 50% on personal orders. The starter kit is $149 (a $600 value) and includes products, catalogs, home show invitations, order forms, promotional flyers, a training guide, training materials on video and audio cassettes, and a searchable CD-ROM.

Aularale Cosmetics

Aularale Cosmetics, 4025 Welcome All Road, Suite 115, Atlanta, GA 30349. Tel: 404-349-7145 or 800-969-8869. Fax: 404-346-7499. E-mail: aularale@aol.com. Web: www.aularale.com.

Aularale Cosmetics is a direct sales cosmetics company. Based in Atlanta, Georgia, the company is owned by the husband and wife team of Alton and Joanne Trawick, who started the company in 1984 from their home with only seven products. The company now has thousands of Beauty Consultants all over the United States and in several foreign countries. Beauty Consultants earn up to 50% commission on personal sales and up to 8% on recruit commissions. The starter kit is $150, which includes the manual, order forms, training support program, a selection of 33 products, sales aids and supplies. Aularale has a company car program for consultants with 15 personal recruits and $4,000 sales volume per month. They also offer special commissions for fundraising sales and prize incentives.

Avon

Avon Products, Inc. Headquarters, 1251 Avenue of the Americas, New York, NY 10020. Tel: 800-367-2866 or 212-282-7000. Web: www.avon.com

Avon is among the power direct selling agencies. They offer skin care products and gifts and they've been in business for more than 100 years! Consultants earn between 25–50% commission and between 5–12% on team members. The cost to start is only $10, and the starter kit usually is comprised of catalogs, a customer development book, and an order book. Incentives and bonuses include trips, scholarships, car bonuses, free products. Avon has 2.6 million consultants in 135 countries. Training is available once a month with a District Sales Manager. An online shop is available, and trips, scholarships, car bonuses, and free products are among their sales incentives. There are no inventories, quotas, or territories.

Azante Jewelry

Azante Jewelry, P.O. Box 11476, Green Bay, WI 54307. Tel: 866-829-2683. E-mail: cherilarson@azantejewelry.com. Web: www.azantejewelry.com.

Azante Jewelry is designed and selected by Cheri Larson, founder of the company that now sells her jewelry through consultants all over the country. The collection includes freshwater pearls, Swarovski® Austrian crystals, semi-precious gems, Bali Sterling Silver, and more. Consultants earn 25% on personal sales and a monthly commission check on sales from consultants you sponsor. Through their Quick Start program, consultants can earn up to $1,600 in free jewelry during the first 90 days as a consultant. Incentives include free jewelry, cash, and trips. The minimum requirement to become a consultant is to purchase the Business & Training Supplies Package for $99, which includes invitations, catalogs, order forms, display materials, and the company training manual. For jewelry samples, two additional kits are available that contain best-selling items. The Basic Kit is $200 and the Premiere Kit is $500, both of which include jewelry at a discount of 50%. You may also select up to ten additional items at 50% off.

BeautiControl, Inc.**

BeautiControl, Inc., P.O. Box 815189, Dallas, TX 75381-5189. Physical address: 2121 Midway Road, Carrollton, TX 75006. Tel: 800-232-8841. E-mail: clientservices@beauticontrol.com. Web: www.beauticontrol.com.

Founded in 1982, BeautiControl Cosmetics is based in Dallas and is a wholly owned subsidiary of Tupperware Corporation. BeautiControl offers skin care, image, and glamour products and has been in business for 20 years. Consultants earn 40–50% commission on sales and 4–12% on team member sales. The company has more than 50,000 BeautiControl Independent Skin Care and Image Consultants. The starter kit is $99–$250 (depending on specials), containing more than $800 worth of beauty products, literature, business-building services and image training. It also includes one day of classroom training (a $200 value); official certification as a professional Independent Skin Care and Image Consultant; their BeautiCase filled with products, tools and literature; a personalized Web page, free for six months (a $60 value); and a free six-month membership in their direct mail program (a $17.50 value). To remain an active consultant, you must sell $100 retail every 4 months. Bonuses and incentives include trips, jewelry, and cash.

Big Enough

Big Enough, 138 Water Street, S. Norwalk, CT 06854. Tel: 800-288-7321. Fax: 203-855-6391. E-mail: customerservice@bigenough.com.
Web: www.bigenough.com.

Big Enough is a 14-year-old company specializing in sportswear for children ages 1–12 years old. WOW—Worlds of Wardrobing—is their selling system that allows the customer to purchase 4 to 8 mix-and-match pieces of clothing, creating a wardrobe of 4 to 16 outfits. Big Enough reps sell the clothes by hosting trunk shows, or by setting up personal shopping appointments with friends.

For a rep's first two seasons, you receive 15–25 sample pieces of clothing on loan, as well as a display. New reps on this trial period only pay for the sales kit ($40–$60) and shipping of the samples and the display for $17. At the end of the trial period, reps must pay $79 for the display if they want to continue. Plus, each season every rep is required to purchase a sales kit and mandatory samples, plus shipping. Reps earn 10% on sales until they reach $1,999; 25% when they reach $2,000–$7,999; and earn 30% when they reach $8,000 in sales.

Reps who reach $8,000 in sales a season can become Area Manager and hire and train up to 20 reps under her. Area Managers earn 5% of their sales. Area Managers who have at least 5 reps under her, with one becoming Area Manager, then become Regional Director, and earn 2% of her Area Manager's sales.

Reps earn 10% free clothing allowance on their sales, and can purchase up to 25 pieces of anything in the collection at 40% off within the first 30 days of each season.

The Bittersweet Candle Company**

The Bittersweet Candle Company, 5230 Park Emerson Drive, Suite I, Indianapolis, IN 46203. Tel: 317-881-2930. Fax: 317-881-2240. E-mail: sales@bittersweetcandle.com. Web: www.bittersweetcandle.com.

The Bittersweet Candle Company is a family owned direct sales company that hand-makes premium candles. Their reps primarily at-home moms. The company was started by Gene and Heather Kramer as a project in the basement, and in 2000 their first rep began selling the candles. They plan to branch out into handmade spa products in Fall 2004. Independent reps earn up to 30% commission on retail sales. There are no monthly sales quotas and no shipping and handling fees.

Cell Tech**

Cell Tech, 565 Century Court, Klamath Falls, OR 97601. Tel: 541-882-5406. Web: www.celltech.com

Cell Tech markets a product known as Super Blue Green® Algae. The product is a nutritional with many benefits, and the company harvests millions of pounds of algae a year. The Distributor Kit costs less than $100. All new Distributors begin at the Member title, which allows you to be eligible to receive a 5% commission on the purchases you make, and on the purchases made by any recruits you enroll. As you attain higher titles, the percentage you receive on those purchases can increase to a full 25%.

Charmed Moments

P.O. Box 571616, Salt Lake City, Utah 84157. Tel: 801-904-1859. Email: info@charmedmoments.com. Web: www.charmedmoments.com.

Charmed Moments specializes in charm jewelry. The company has hundreds of charms that can be added to bracelets, watches, necklaces toe rings, and earrings. The company has been in business for almost three years, and has about 400 consultants in the U.S. Their main method of sales for the Independent Jewelry Consultants are home parties ("open houses"). Training is available through a training workbook, regional trainings, annual conventions, and personalized training from sponsors. The company plans to offer Web stores to their consultants in the next year.

The basic starter kit is $249 and the deluxe kit is $395. The Basic Kit contains basic display items, business supplies, and charms and jewelry, valued at more than $500. The Deluxe Kit contains the same kinds of items, with a retail value of more than $850. Consultants earn 30–46% commission on sales, depending on promotional level, plus 2–9% on personal recruits. To remain an active consultant, you must sell at least $150 per quarter. Other minimal quotas need to be met monthly to receive downline payments. Incentives include monthly sales awards, cruises and trips, jewelry, and other prizes.

Chic Pursenality

Chic Pursenality, 2404 Callaway Ct., Wentzville, MO 63385. E-mail: info@chicpursenality.com. Web: www.chicpursenality.com.

Chic Pursenality is a direct sales company selling the latest trends in handbags, purses, jewelry, and other accessories. The company was founded in 2002. The company's "Purse Parties" offer consultants a 25% commission on sales, with the potential to make 32%. To sign up is $25, and starter kits are additional. The Basic Starter Kit is $98 and contains approximately seven handbags, the handbook, paperwork, invitations, and 50 business cards. The Starter Kit is $150 and contains approximately twelve handbags, the handbook, paperwork, invitations, and 50 business cards. (For both kits you may suggest which bags you want included.) The company also offers consultants 50% off items, sale specials, and sales incentives. There are no minimum downline requirements. As long as you are an active consultant, you receive commissions on any amount of consultants you have recruited.

Close to My Heart

Close to My Heart, 1199 West 700 South, Pleasant Grove, UT 84062. Tel: 888-655-6552. Fax: 800-637-8615. Web: www.closetomyheart.com.

Close to My Heart sells rubber stamps, papers, inks, and scrapbooking supplies. The consultant kit is $89.95, which includes a Display Board Kit, with all the stamps, inks, accessories, and instructions you need to create cards and layouts to share at "Home Gatherings." The kit contains more than $220 worth of products. The annual fee to remain a consultant is $20. Consultants earn between 22–32% commission and an additional 2% on team members. Incentives include trips and monthly goody bags for sales over $2,000.

Cookie Lee Jewelry

17791 Sky Park Circle, Suite D, Irvine, CA 92614. Tel: 949-252-0335. Fax: 949-252-0455. Email: info@cookielee.com. Web: www.cookielee.com.

Cookie Lee began selling jewelry to her friends and family in 1985. In 1992, Cookie Lee Jewelry was offered as a direct sales company to the public. Inspired by contemporary designs and classic jewelry basics, Cooke Lee jewelry is sold through home shows, office shows, fundraisers, and personal shopping through independent consultants. Consultants earn 50% commission on sales. Incentives include all-expense-paid trips and jewelry purchases and sponsoring help consultants accumulate "Successorize" points towards logo merchandise and business supplies. There is no kit to purchase—consultants select the jewelry they would like to sell.

Country Bunny Bath and Body**

Country Bunny Bath and Body, 1106 Eaglecrest, Nixa, MO 65714. Tel: 877-665-8669 or 417-724-9690. E-mail: atyourservice@cbunny.com. Web: www.cbunny.com.

Country Bunny specializes in bath and body products created with recipes by Founder and Owner Nancy Bogart. Independent Representatives ("Bunnies") can join Country Bunny Bath & Body for $179, which includes the company's corporate support service, a free Web site for one year, an online training center, corporate training, and a starter kit containing catalogs and products. Bunnies can sell at Spa Shows, crafts fairs, and online. Training is provided through monthly training calls and an annual convention ("Bunnyvention"). Representatives earn 15% commission on sales, plus 5–10% on downline sales. Country Bunny has been in business since 2000.

Creative Memories

Creative Memories, 3001 Clearwater Road, P.O. Box 1839, St. Cloud, MN 56302-1839. Tel: 800-341-5275. Fax: 800-605-2454. E-mail: us@creative-memories.com. Web: www.creativememories.com.

Creative Memories was founded in 1987 in St. Cloud, Minnesota, by Cheryl Lightle and Rhonda Anderson. Since its inception, Creative Memories has become a multi-national company with more than 60,000 consultants worldwide. Creative Memories Consultants teach the importance of and techniques for organizing, documenting, and preserving photographs and memorabilia in safe, meaningful, keepsake albums. Consultants educate and provide hands-on assistance during home classes, workshops, and other events. Creative Memories provides a step-by-step start-up program and support materials designed to make it easy to become a Creative Memories Consultant. Their Consultant Kit is $195 and includes business supplies and a selection of materials (a $500 value). Consultants earn 30–45% commission, plus 3–12% commission on downline sales.

DeMarle At Home**

DeMarle at Home, 5601 West Slauson Ave, Suite 160, Culver City, CA 90230. Tel: 310-568-1717. Fax: 310-568-8748. Web: www.demarleathome.com.

DeMarle at Home specializes in kitchen gadgets, tools, and accessories aimed at making creative cooking simple. DeMarle at Home specializes in the "Flexipan," a unique nonstick baking pan. DeMarle Representatives demonstrate these products at home parties called "Rendex-Vous." DeMarle at Home has approximately 5,150 representatives worldwide. The starter kit is $149.95 with an opportunity to receive a 49.95 reimbursement within the first 40 days of their initial start date. Starter kit includes 10 products, including a flower mold flexipan, large muffin tray, medium silpat, stainless mixing bowl, ergonomic whisk, heat resistant spatula, beechwood rolling pin, and recipe binder with cards. Also included are marketing materials, including catalogs, brochures, and training video. Commissions are 20–31% on sales, plus 2–11% commission override on recruits.

Discovery Toys**

Discovery Toys, Tel: 800-426-4777. E-mail: contactdt@discoverytoys.net. Web: www.discoverytoysinc.com.

Discovery Toys is about "kid powered play." They specialize in toys and games that are educational, developmental, and fun. The company has been in business for more than 25 years, and has expanded into a line of books and software. DT's Educational Consultants earn 25–50% commission on sales and 7–15% on team members. The Intro Kit costs $149 (although they offer discounted kits often) with fourteen of their best-selling products, as well as 25 catalogs and all of the supplies and training materials you'll need to get started.

Ecoquest International

EcoQuest International, 310 T. Elmer Cox Drive, Greeneville, TN 37743. Tel: 800-486-4994. Fax: 423-638-7561. E-mail: customerservice@ecoquestintl.com. Web: www.ecoquestintl.com.

EcoQuest is a company dedicated to enhancing the quality of life indoors. EcoQuest products include air purification products, nutritional products, personal care products, herbals, and household products. Ecoquest is a 45-year-old Fortune 500 company. Representatives earn 16–42% commission on sales. Bonuses include a travel and expense program; a company car program; profit-sharing; trips; and group sales bonuses to the seventh generation. The Success Pack includes 5 BreezeAT units, 1 Fresh Air, 1 Living Proof, sales and recruiting boxes, literature, training audio and video tapes, and more, and costs $2,395. The company operates in the U.S., UK, Australia, and Taiwan.

Enchanted Potions

Enchanted Potions, 8490 Community Place, Ooltewah, TN 37363. Tel: 423-499-6438. Fax: 217-345-0439. E-mail: epcustomerservice@comcast.net. Web: www.enchantedpotions.com.

Enchanted Potions creates handmade soaps and bath products. With a large variety of products and more than 90 fragrances to choose from. Bath products include Mystical Bath Salts, Divine Garden Sprite soaps, fragrant Moonmist shower gel, and Stardust bubble bath. The company has been in business for four years, but has been crafting bath and body products since 1997. There are approximately 140 consultants operating in U.S., Canada, Germany, Japan, and Belgium. Their Distributors sell at "Enchanted Gatherings" (home parties). Training is provided by team leaders, with the aid of sales incentives and company literature. To remain active, distributors must make a purchase quarterly. To be eligible for downline commissions, distributors must make one monthly purchase of any dollar amount. They offer two main incentive programs, the Stardust Ladder Program which offers increased commissions for team leaders, and the Stardust Point Program which offers points from sales, purchases, recruiting, and more that can be redeemed for prizes.

Distributors earn a base commission of 30%, plus a 5% commission on team members (first generation only). The starter kit is $10, and contains a training manual on CD and product samples. They also offer a free start-up plan where distributors must make a purchase for any dollar amount within 30 days to sign up. Party invitations, hostess flyers, and product catalogs are available a low cost per item.

Enchanting Scents Designs**

Enchanting Scents Designs, 1510 Easton Avenue, Madison, OH 44057. Tel: 440-428-3961. Fax: 530-463-8637. E-mail: escents@ncweb.com. Web: www.esdsoycandles.com.

Enchanting Scents Designs (ESD) is a direct selling company specializing in custom designed candles. Their candles are made from 100% natural soy wax. Each Candle is triple scented which allows the scent to last hours after the candle is extinguished. Enchanting Scents Designs, located in rural Madison, Ohio, was founded in the spring of 1998. The company have grown to distribute their products across the United States and Canada through its 100 distributors. Distributors earn 30–33% commission on sales, plus 3% on downline sales. The starter kit is free, and includes a training manual and business documents.

FemOne**

FemOne, 5600 Avenida Encinas, Suite 130, Carlsbad, CA 92008. Tel: 760-448-2498. Fax: 760-454-4511. E-mail: support@femone.com. Web: www.femone.com.

FemOne sells nutritionals, cosmetics, and weight loss products that balance and enhance health and beauty. The company has been in business since 2002. FemOne Consultants receive a 30% discount on products, a personalized e-commerce Web site to sell retail products, and a virtual office to order business cards and organize contacts. Senior consultants earn 15% on first generation recruits, and 5% on second generation recruits. There are two options to become a FemOne Business Associate. The Welcome Kit is $24.95 and contains the Welcome Binder only. The $49.95 kit adds an assortment of products. The FemOne Consultant Manager Kit is $1,000 and contains approximately $1,447 worth of products as well as the FemOne Welcome Binder that contains company and product information, order forms, and training materials.

For Your Pleasure, Inc.**

For Your Pleasure, Inc., P.O. Box 3452, Concord, NH 03302. Tel: 603-225-8826 Fax: 603-225-3199 Email: info@foryourpleasure.com.
Web:www.foryourpleasure.com

For Your Pleasure began as Rainbow Resource, a New Hampshire-based company providing online and mail order products to the adult community. Due to increasing requests for an intimate setting for demonstrating products, lotions, and novelties, the wholesale home party division was born and began hosting For Your Pleasure Parties in 1999. The starter kit can be purchased for $250, $500, or $1,000, each containing products worth double the kit price. Consultants (FYP Independent Business Associate) can also earn the kit for free through an "Open For Business Show."

Associates receive up to 50% commission from home shows, direct sales, and online sales. They can also earn up to another 10% for bonus in a month, based on sales, not recruits. Associates can earn up to 10% on first line recruits, plus overrides on second, third, fourth, and fifth. Bonuses of up to $1,500 on downline sales are available as well.

The Fuller Brush Company**

The Fuller Brush Company, One Fuller Way, Great Bend, KS 67530. Tel: 800-522-0499. Fax: 620-792-1906. E-mail: info@fuller.com. Web: www.fuller.com.

Fuller Brush is a home care company. Through the years, The Fuller Brush Company has grown from one man's fiber suitcase, filled with unique custom-made brushes, to a collection of home/business care, and personal care products. More than 2,000 items are formed within their twelve-acre plant including: household cleaning aids, industrial cleaners, polishes & wax products, cotton & synthetic mops, floor brushes & brooms, stainless steel sponges, personal care brushes, lotions and fragrances, hair care aids, and more. The 500,000 square foot plant was completed in 1973, and today Fuller remains the major employer in the Barton County, Kansas area. Consultants earn 20–46% commission on sales, plus 1–26% on downline sales. The starter kits range from free to $39.95, depending on products included.

Gabby Goodies**

Gabby Goodies, Crestwood, IL. Tel: 877-576-7666.
E-mail: gabbygoodies@aol.com. Web: www.gabbygoodies.com

Mary Kuipers founded Gabby Goodies in 2001. After beginning the business as a gift basket enterprise, she discovered that most people wanted the food products available for purchase separately rather than in a basket. She came up with a gourmet foods and coffee business, one that now has almost 350 products being sold though a party plan format. Their product line includes gourmet dip mixes, beer bread mixes, gourmet coffee, cocoa mixes, creamers, brownie mixes, cookies, tea, breads, muffins, and soups.

There are now more than 650 consultants nationwide who market Gabby Goodies in various ways including home parties, craft fairs, gift baskets, school bazaars, and Web sites. Consultants choose which methods work best for them. Consultants receive 25% commission based on their paid sales and there are no minimums to meet. They can advance into field management levels by sponsoring other consultants and in return may qualify for free products based on monthly group sales and number of people they've sponsored. There are two starter kits that contain both product and paperwork, ranging from $29.95–$49.95. There are eight levels of upper level consultants, beginning at Consultant Coordinator and ending at Shining Star Consultant. When each level is attained, free product is awarded. The annual renewal fee if $15.

Gifted Expressions**

Gifted Expressions, 20–28 Sargeant Street, Hartford, CT 06105. Tel: 866-543-4438. Fax: 866-450-5566. E-mail: customerservice@giftedexpressions.com. Web: www.giftedexpressions.com.

Gifted Expressions offers a selection of gourmet food gifts, spa assortments, and accessories. Gift Specialists do not have to purchase and stock any inventory or deliver any orders. All products are shipped from their 25,000 square-foot facility in Hartford, Connecticut within 24–48 hours. "GifTogethers" are their version of the traditional home party. Consultants earn 20% commission on sales, plus 2–7% on recruits. The starter kit is $249 (a $900 retail value) and includes gifting samples, catalogs, brochures, invitations, a training guide, and order forms. Gifted Expressions has been in business since 2003, but their parent company, Giftcorp, has been in business for 20 years.

Girls Night In

Girls Night In, P.O. Box 231735, Encinitas, CA 92023-1735. Tel: 877-464-4968. Fax: 888-846-4329. E-mail: info@shopgirlsnightin.com.
Web: www.shopgirlsnightin.com.

Girls Night In sells clothing, home décor, handbags, spa products, and jewelry. For $25 consultants receive 35 catalogs and a complete "how-to" guide to selling GNI products. Catalog consultants earn 20% on all sales up to $500 in a one month period, and 25% commission on all sales over $501 in a one month period. Commission eligibility starts on the first day of every month and goes through the last day of each month. If you purchase inventory, you can earn up to 50% by selling products on a cash-and-carry basis at parties.

The Gold Canyon Candle Company

Gold Canyon Candle Company. Web: www.goldcanyoncandle.com.

Gold Canyon Candle Company sells candles and candleholders. The company offers two levels of consultant: Demonstrator, who earns 17% commission on sales; and Distributor, who earns 40% on her own sales, plus 17% on their demonstrators' sales. The starter kit for Demonstrators is $130 and contains sample candles. Distributorships can be purchased for $5,000 and may be resold. Gold Canyon Candle Co. began in 1997.

The Good Nature Company

The Good Nature Company, 12137 3 1/2 Mile Rd., Battle Creek, MI 49015. Tel: 269-979-1151. Fax: 269-979-1615. E-mail: jlbeckgoodnature@earthlink.net. Web: www.thegoodnatureco.com.

The Good Nature Company sells landscape ornaments; garden tools and accessories; bird feeders and houses; bat, butterfly and ladybug houses; squirrel feeders; high-quality chimes; educational books, gift items; and indoor décor such as plant rooters, note cards, coaster sets, doormats, clocks, and mugs. Their Business Kit is $150 (a retail value of more than $300). Consultants earn 25% commission, with the chance to earn 30% with sponsoring bonuses. Qualified Consultants (who hold at least four shows with sales of $150 or more) also receive a 30% discount on all personal purchases.

Greta's Bake At Home Cookies

Greta's Bake at Home Cookies, 90 S. Newtown Street Road, Suite 11, Newtown, Square PA 19073. Web: www.bakeathomecookies.com.

Greta is well-known for her cookies throughout northeastern Pennsylvania and Southern Ontario, Canada. Her cookie mixes are now available through consultants and come in eight varieties: Cappuccino Chocolate Chip, Chocolate Chip, Ebony & Ivory Chip, Peanut Butter & Chocolate Chip, Butterscotch & Chocolate Chip, Oatmeal Raisin, Oatmeal Chocolate Chip, and Oatmeal Raisin & Chocolate Chip. Consultants may purchase mixes at the wholesale price of $4.50 and sell them for $7.00 each. In addition, consultants earn 6% commission on first level recruits and 3% on second level.

The initial cost is $135, which includes 30 cookie mixes (a value of $228). This includes two sample packages (enough for 4 batches of cookies) for making cookie samples. Future sample batches are available to consultants at a discount. Greta's signup kit also includes *Instructions on How to Organize Your Parties and*

Recruit New Consultants, a template for printing post card invitations, and a template for printing a Bulletin Board Poster. Consultants then sell the cookie mixes through "cookie baking demonstrations."

HENN Workshops

HENN Workshops, 1001 Country Way, Warren, OH 44481. Tel: 800-BE-A-HENN or 330-824-2575. Fax: 330-824-3637. Web: www.hennworkshops.com.

HENN Workshops specializes in pottery, baskets, candles, and collectibles. Their Spongeware Pottery is crafted in the traditions of historic New Waterford, Ohio, home of the HENN Pottery. The company also produces traditionally crafted baskets and candles. Over the past 20 years, HENN has grown into an international company with consultants all over the world. With nearly 2,200 consultants, they distribute three catalogs each year. Consultants and Leaders have a variety of training opportunities, including annual events. Consultants earn 25% commission on sales. The New Consultant Success Kit is $99.99 (a $184 value) and includes product samples and paperwork. Training is offered through "Career Track Coaches," weekly e-mail training for new consultants, and career building events.

Herbalife International, Inc.**

Herbalife International of America, Inc., P.O. Box 80210, Los Angeles, CA 90080-0210. Tel: 866-866-4744. Fax: 310-258-7019. Web: www.herbalife.com.

Herbalife Distributors begin with the Herbalife International Business Pack (IBP), which costs less than $100 and includes a training manual. Herbalife's products fall into two main categories: "Inner Nutrition," which includes weight loss, essential nutrition, health supplements; energy boosters, and fitness and sports snacks/nutrition products; and "Outer Nutrition," which includes skin care and hair care products. The products are aimed at slimming down, increasing energy, de-stressing, and rejuvenating skin. Independent Distributors are trained to create customized programs for their customers, based on their Cellular Nutrition® approach. Herbalife was founded in 1980, and now has more than one million independent distributors selling Herbalife products in 58 countries worldwide (and annual retail sales of $1.8 billion).

Herbalife's distributor training and support system includes: monthly success training seminars; leadership development weekends; televised product and business-building training via the Herbalife Broadcast Network; Internet support tools; annual international events for networking and training; advice from the Herbalife Medical Advisory Board and Medical Affairs Group; sales literature and promotional tools; and access to wellness training seminars. Herbalife Distributors earn 25–50% commission, plus 5–25% on team members.

Highlights Jigsaw

Highlights Jigsaw, 1800 Watermark Drive, Columbus, OH 43215. Tel: 800-934-4689 or 614-324-7902. Web: www.highlightsjigsaw.com.

Highlights Jigsaw is a unique partnership between *Highlights* magazine, the successful children's magazine for 50 years, and the Jigsaw Toy Factory, a successful direct selling party-plan educational toy company in Australia for more than 30 years. Their motto is "Fun with a Purpose!" and they market products that develop playing, learning and reading skills, creativity and imagination, and social skills and confidence through positive messages and values, non-violent play, and family fun. Products include *Highlights* magazine, puzzle books, activities, and CD-ROMs; Jigsaw's toys games, puzzles, and posters; Boyds Mills Press (a division of Highlights) picture books, and fiction and non-fiction books; and ELP (a division of Highlights) skill-guided practice books for reading, writing, math, and more.

Their version of a home party are "Talkabouts," and consultants can also sell at pre-schools, daycares, schools, and at "Toyraisers" (their version of a fundraiser). Consultants earn 20–34% commission on retail checks as well as 6% on team members, as well as a 3% lifetime sponsoring bonus (and total of 9% on recruits). The Business Kit costs between $49–$149 (depending on specials) and includes 22 of their best-selling toys and games. Products are sent directly to customers, and the company provides free phone conference training.

Home and Garden Party**

Home and Garden Party, Ltd. 2938 Brown Rd., Marshall, TX 75672. Tel: 903-935-4197. Fax: 903-935-3170. E-mail: customerservice@hgcorp.net. Web: www.homeandgardenparty.com.

Home & Garden Party is a home-based party plan business featuring home décor items such as hand-turned stoneware pottery, framed prints, terracotta pottery, figurines, brass accessories, home décor items, candles and fragrances, bath gels and lotions, and kitchenware. Home and Garden Party's Designers have an initial start-up cost is $150, which includes a selection of Home and Garden Party products, as well as catalogs, order forms, instruction booklets, videos, and supplies (a retail value of $300). They offer a guaranteed one-year buy-back option if you leave the business. Designers earn 30% to 40% of commission plus 3–6% override commissions on recruits.

Homemade Gourmet

Homemade Gourmet, Tel: 888-477-2848.
E-mail: distributorrelations@homemadegourmet.com.
Web: www.homemadegourmet.com.

Homemade Gourmet's mission is to "remedy the deterioration of the family dinner hour," drawing America's families back to the table by providing "delicious, affordable, and easy-to-make" mixes. Their mixes are available through their Independent Distributors. Distributors purchase product at wholesale prices and resell them to their customers at suggested retail prices, which are printed in the catalog. Their preferred sales venues are through home shows, re-orders, and meal planning classes. The sponsorship process includes signing a Distributor Agreement and purchasing a $99.00 starter kit that includes enough mixes to sample at three parties (30 products), plus business supplies.

Homemade Gourmet Team Leaders (Sponsors) are responsible for training and supporting their new teams. As teams grow, compensation also increases, as distributors a receive a monthly percentage of their team's sales. Distributors earn 10–20% commission on sales.

The Homemaker's Idea Company**

The Homemaker's Idea Company, 500 Wall St., Glendale Heights, IL 60139. Tel: 800-800-5452. E-mail: info@homemakersidea.com.
Web: www.homemakersideacompany.com.

For more than 32 years, The Homemaker's Idea Company has been selling a line of organizing and decorating essentials, including baskets, linens, florals, greens, pottery, and wallpaper borders through home parties. Products come under several categories: Casual Living; Bridal and Inspiration; Bathin' Beauty; Entertain in Style; Romantic Spaces; Store 'n' More; Comfortable Classics; Escape from the Ordinary; Kid's Style; and That Extra Touch. Consultants earn 25% commission of retail sales, plus 2–5% commission on downline sales, depending on consultant level and recruit generation. The starter case is $175 (and can go as low as $100 on special), and can be returned within one year for a 90% refund. The kit contains $500 worth of retail products and business supplies.

HomeWare Creations**

HomeWare Creations, Administrative Office, 447 Fulton Street, Suite 200, Waverly, NY 14901. Tel: 607-565-8953. Fax: 607-565-8991.
E-mail: contactus@homewarecreations.com.
Web: www.homewarecreations.com.

HomeWare Creations opened its doors in March 2003, and has been under new management since February 2004. Its business opportunity is scheduled to relaunch in July 2004. They presently have 100 Associates in 30 states. There are three levels of Associate: Associate, Lead Associate, and Director. Associates earn 20% commission, while Fundraiser Specialists earn 15% commission. In addition, Associates may purchase products at 50% off and earn 3% commission on first line recruit sales. Homeware Creations has a free start-up option where you commit to four home parties and that from the third and fourth party commissions you repay $125 to offset the cost of the startup kit (which is a $300 value).

Jafra Cosmetics International

Jafra Cosmetics International, 2451 Townsgate Rd., Westlake Village, CA 91361. Tel: 800-551-2345. E-mail: customercare@jafra.com. Web: www.jafra.com.

In 1956, Jan and Frank Day founded Jafra out of their home in Malibu, California. Jafra Cosmetics has been in business for 45 years. Jafra Cosmetics International now has an international network of nearly 400,000 women in 22 countries. Their products include skin care, fragrance, color products (cosmetics), body products (bath salts, massage cream, oils and lotion), and family products (sun and hair care). Their Web site has a helpful marketing tool: an online skin care quiz for potential customers to see which Jafra products they would recommend for your particular skin type. Consultants earn up to 50% commission on sales. The starter kit includes a Jafra tote and sales tools.

Joielle Fine Jewelry**

Joielle Fine Jewelry. Tel: 866-994-7370. Web: www.joielle.com.

Joielle® (pronounced JOY-EL) is a manufacturer and distributor of fine jewelry. The name Joielle means "bringing joy to her." The company was founded by Michael Posternak and his two brothers, Martin and Daniel who wanted to start a new business that would create high quality, fashionable, affordable fine jewelry to be distributed through independent Jewelry Consultants at home demonstrations. The Joielle collection consists of 400 fine jewelry pieces handcrafted by worldwide designers in sterling silver and accented with 14k gold, gemstones, and pearls. The Joielle designer signature is featured on the jewelry collections.

Consultants earn 25% to 40% commission on jewelry sales, plus 2.5% to 20% on team members. The business kit costs $120, and includes one of their most popular bangle bracelets, a pair of earrings, and a piece of peridot; Joielle first year registration; a Joielle home page; access to the consultant Web site; Joielle catalogs; invitation postcards; Joielle gift box and roll; anti-tarnish velvet pouches; opportunity brochures; hostess and guest order forms; registration agreements; the consultant "Guide to Success" manual; a ring sizer; plus a one-time discount on demonstration jewelry, up to 65% off retail.

Lady Remington Jewelry

Lady Remington Jewelry, Bensenville, IL. Tel: 800-487-3323. E-mail: cs@ladyremingtonjewelry.com. Web: www.ladyremingtonjewelry.com.

Lady Remington is a direct selling opportunity offering jewelry and fashion accessorizing through personalized in-home demonstrations. Consultants earn 30–40% commission on sales. For more than 30 years their home office has been located in Bensenville, Illinois.

Leaving Prints™

Leaving Prints™, 1753 West Business Park Dr., Orem, Utah 84058. Tel: 801-426-0636. Fax: 801-434-8877. E-mail: careeropportunity@leavingprints.com. Web: www.leavingprints.com.

Leaving Prints is a direct selling scrapbooking company. The company was launched in 2003 and has 2,800 consultants in the U.S. Leaving Prints Instructors conduct "Learn and Earn" classes to sell LP products. Instructors earn up to 43% commission on sales, plus up to 18% on downline sales. Instructors must purchase $75 per quarter to purchase product at wholesale prices. Training is available through area and regional trainings and an annual convention. The starter kit is $25 and includes a training manual. Both *Simple Scrap* magazine and *Creating Keepsakes* magazine have featured LP products.

The Limu Company

The Limu Company, 610 Crescent Executive Court, Suite 110, Lake Mary, FL 32746. Tel: 407-804-1044. Fax: 407-804-8275.
E-mail: info@thelimucompany.com. Web: www.thelimucompany.com.

The Limu Company sells a natural health supplement, Original Limu™. For thousands of years, generations of Tongans handed down the ancient secret of Limu Moui, a sea plant growing abundantly in the waters of the South Pacific. Limu Moui contains a storehouse of vitamins, minerals, antioxidants, amino acids, and glyconutrients. But of the 70 plus substances found in Limu Moui, the one that is most important, according to the company, is fucoidan. The company has an exclusive agreement with the Kingdom of Tonga to harvest Limu Moui, and has spent 15 years perfecting the extraction process to produce their Limu extract. Limu Moui grows in abundance in the ocean just off the Islands of Tonga and renews itself naturally.

Customers can purchase Original Limu™ from a distributor at retail for $42 per bottle, or they may become members for $25 and purchase it at wholesale for $35 per bottle. Members may also choose TLC's Limu Case Qualified (LCQ) program, which gives you 4 bottles for $120.

The company was previously known as Royal Tongan Limu by Dynamic Essentials, and was re-established in August 2003 under the new name of The Limu Company. The company has 25,000 distributors worldwide. The starter kit is $25 (with a yearly renewal fee of the same) and contains paperwork and manuals to introduce the product and sign up new members. Training is provided by the manual and the upline sponsor.

Longaberger

One Market Square, 1500 East Main street, Newark, OH 43055-8847. Tel: 800-966-0374 or 740-322-5000. Fax: 740-322-5240. Web: www.longaberger.com.

Thirty years ago, Dave Longaberger founded The Longaberger Company with five basket makers. Today they are considered "the nation's premier maker of handcrafted baskets," and now also specialize in home and lifestyle products including pottery and wrought iron and fabric accessories. The company has nearly 70,000 consultants in the U.S. There are three starter kits to choose from, each containing a selection of products, supplies, and business-building tools. The Business Basics Kit is $99 (a $280 value); the Business on the Go Kit is $249 (a $490 value); and the Business Builder Kit is $399 (a $760 value). Longaberger consultants earn 25% commission on sales. Consultants receive $200 in Longaberger products for every new qualified recruit. Sales field leaders earn additional compensation and override commissions on team members. Training is available through an annual sales convention, online seminars, regional training events, and publications. In 2003 Longaberger received the DSA Vision for Tomorrow Award for its community service efforts to substantially improve the quality of life in communities.

Mary Kay Cosmetics**

Mary Kay Cosmetics Inc., P.O. Box 799045, Dallas, TX 75379-9045. Tel: 800-627-9529. Web: www.marykay.com.

The Mary Kay World Headquarters is located in North Dallas and totals nearly 600,000 square feet. Approximately 3,600 Mary Kay Inc. employees serve more than 1.1 million Independent Beauty Consultants and their customers in more than 30 markets worldwide. Mary Kay is one of the largest direct sellers of skin care and color cosmetics in the world. The Mary Kay® product line includes more than 200 products in seven categories: facial skin care, color cosmetics, nail care, body care, sun protection, fragrances and men's skin care.

Mary Kay's starter kit costs $100 (a $400 retail value) and includes a product demonstration kit and educational materials. Independent Beauty Consultants also have access to their own Mary Kay Web site. Incentives include computer equipment, trips, and its legendary Career Car Program that includes nearly 10,000 U.S. cars. Facials and skin care classes are the main method of selling products. Reps earn 50% commission and 4–26% on downline sales.

Melaleuca, Inc.

Melaleuca, Inc., 3910 S. Yellowstone Hwy, Idaho Falls, ID 83402. Tel: 800-742-2444 or 208-522-0700. Fax: 888-528-2090. E-mail: info@melaleuca.com. Web: www.melaleuca.com.

Melaleuca sells non-toxic personal and home care products and skin care and nutritional supplements. The company has been in business for 16 years, and operates in the U.S., Japan, Taiwan, Australia, Canada, and Hong Kong. Consultants earn 20% commission, plus 7% overrides and bonuses. The starter kit is $29 and contains information about their products.

MemoryWorks

MemoryWorks, P.O. Box 346, Roy, Utah 84067. Tel: 801-985-0357. Fax: 801-985-3045. E-mail: info@memory-works.com. Web: www.memory-works.com.

MemoryWorks sells scrapbooking supplies. The company was launched in October 2002 and now has more than 325 Independent Scrapbook Consultants that sell through "Memories and Moments Scrapbook Workshops." The company operates in the continental U.S., the U.S. Territories, Alaska, Hawaii, and overseas military. Consultant Kit is $65, plus a $15 consultant locater fee, and includes a business binder, manual, invitations, business forms, business cards, and a $50 product credit. Training is provided through the manual, online support, workshops, newsletter, consultant chat room, the consultant support team. Consultants earn 20% commission on sales and a 20% personal discount. MemoryWorks is a single-level direct sales business unit and is not comprised of multi-levels. Although you are not required to recruit new consultants, consultants are rewarded with a $15 MemoryWorks product credit for each new consultant recruited. There are no monthly minimums or quarterly sales quotas to meet.

My Precious Kid**

My Precious Kid™, P.O. Box 271, Banks, OR 97106-0271.Tel: 503-324-7323. Fax: 775-667-6323. E-mail: Kay@mypreciouskid.com.
Web: www.MyPreciousKid.com.

My Precious Kid specializes in ID cards for children that provide basic medical information, fingerprints, and emergency contact information, as well as a medical release signature. The $30 initial package for reps contains one $16 sample Child Safety Pack, as well as a flyer, order form, catalog, name tag, product display board, sales manual, calendar, promo order form, mileage log, stickers and sample letters. The $30 also covers the cost of setting up your rep account and wholesale buying status. The optional additional New Rep Sample Pack is $94 and contains one of each of their 17 products (a $188.00 value).

Reps can buy any of their ID card products wholesale (50% off retail) and resell them to the customers when you buy the $50 minimum ($100 retail). Consultants receive 25% profit on smaller orders and on drop-shipped orders. Profit on non-ID-kit items (not made by MPK) is 25–30%. There is a 5% commission on recruits. In order to receive downline commissions, reps must have order $50 wholesale each month.

NEST Family

NEST Family, 1461 S. Beltline Rd., Suite 500, Coppell, TX 75019. Tel: 800-447-5958 or 972-402-7100. E-mail: salessupport@nestfamily.com. Web: www.nestfamily.com.

NestFamily sells inspirational, educational, and entertaining video and audio collections for families. Their products are available on DVD, videocassette, audio CDs, and cassettes and focus on Bible and hero stories. In addition, the company distributes the award-winning computer animated series for preschoolers, *Jay Jay The Jet Plane* from PorchLight Entertainment and Modern Cartoons.

NestFamily independent distributors have access to their own e-commerce Web site and other business building tools, including personalized e-mail capability, online ordering, sponsoring, automated order and shipping e-mail confirmations.

Northern Lights at Home**

Northern Lights at Home 3474 Andover Road, Wellsville, NY 14895. Tel: 585-593-1200. Fax: 585-593-6481. E-mail: info@northernlightsathome.com. Web: www.northernlightsathome.com.

Northern Lights at Home was founded in 1978 by Andres and Christina Glanzman when they produced original wax designs in their small Western New York workshop and marketed them at local art and craft shows. Today, NLAH sells candles through independent presenters and the At Home Division is now represented in 41 states. They offer their Presenters ongoing training and business-building ideas and aids. All their products have a 30 day money-back guarantee. Presenters earn 30% commission on sales, plus a 5% monthly bonus. Incentives include gifts and vacations. In 2003 the company celebrated its 25th anniversary.

Nouveau Cosmeceuticals**

Nouveau Cosmeceuticals, 1746 West Crosby Road, Carrollton, TX 75006. Tel: 877-296-6883. Web: www.bynouveau.com.

Nouveau Cosmeceuticals offers a skin care line and wellness products. Consultants earn 45% in commissions, plus 4–8% on downline sales. The Executive Starter Kit is $249 (a retail value of more than $450) and includes a Consultant ID number, online manual, 2 complete Nouveau Systems, 2 Nouveau Slimming and Regenerating Body Systems, 25 Nouveau Cosmeceutical Brochures, 25 Nouveau Body Cosmeceutical Brochures, the option to enroll in the autoship program, and sample products. The Basic Starter Kit is $49.95 and includes consultant ID number, online manual, and the option to enroll in the autoship program. The company has been in business since 2002.

Nu Skin International**

Nu Skin International, Inc., One NuSkin Plaza, 75 West Center Street, Provo, UT 84601. Tel: 801-345-1000. Fax: 801-345-2799. E-mail: contactus@nuskin.com. Web: www.nuskin.com.

Founded in 1984, Nu Skin has expanded into more than 30 markets worldwide with more than 550,000 active distributors selling personal care products. They specialize in skin care, ethnobotanicals, hair care, cosmetics, fragrance, and oral care products. Nu Skin has a network of more than 550,000 independent sales representatives in more than 30 countries. Distributors earn 25–33% commission on sales, plus 6–12% on downline sales. The starter kit is $99–$398, depending on products included.

Once Upon a Charm...®**

Once Upon A Charm...®, P.O. Box 971152, Orem, UT 84097. Tel: 866-6CHARMS or 801-370-3482. Fax: 801-607-3416.
E-mail: onceuponacharm@comcast.net. Web: www.onceuponacharm.com.

Once Upon A Charm...® sells sterling silver charms and bracelets. Founded in Provo, Utah, Once Upon A Charm...® is a nationwide direct sales company offering more than 1,200 sterling silver charms to choose from, a variety of sterling silver bracelets, necklaces, and their Once Upon A Charm...® Storybook™.

The starter kit is $130 and includes 20 product samples of their most popular charms, 2 sample bracelets, 12 catalogs, a display system, and the paperwork you need to start your business. Commission on sales is 22%, with 2–3% on down-line sales. Training is provided through the consultant manual, monthly consultant news, meetings, and upline training. Incentives include products and business tools for monthly sales volumes. Once Upon A Charm...® has been in business since 2001.

Once Upon a Family**

Once Upon a Family, 17252 Armstrong Ave, Suite B, Irvine, CA 92614. Tel: 949-250-1155. Fax: 949-955-0665. Web: www.onceuponafamily.com.

Once Upon a Family specializes in specialty scrapbooks, albums, and family tree accessories. The products include baby books, journals, family tree books, note cards, scrapbooks, holiday photo books, and specialty items. Consultants earn up to 25% commission at "Celebrations," (home shows). Bonuses can range from 2% to 8%. Other incentives include free products, spa weekends, and cruises. Consultants also have the opportunity to achieve "Honorary Founder" status based on their sales. There are several starter kits to choose from, ranging from $125 to $370. Training is available through upline sponsors, corporate training staff, teleconference calls, and weekend events. Once Upon a Family has been in business since 2002.

The Pampered Chef

The Pampered Chef, One Pampered Chef Lane, Addison, Illinois 60101-5630. Tel: 800-266-5562 or 630-261-8900. Fax: 630-261-8522. Web: www.pamperedchef.com

The Pampered Chef has been selling high-quality kitchen tools for almost 25 years. Consultants earn 20% commission on sales, plus 3% on team members. Products are sold primarily through in-home cooking demonstrations known as Kitchen Shows. The cost to start is $100, which includes $350 worth of kitchen tools and paperwork for six parties. There are no annual fees to remain a consultant.

The Pampered Chef has more than 70,000 independent Kitchen Consultants across the United States, Canada, the United Kingdom, and Germany. Chairman and Founder Doris Christopher is the author of *Come to the Table* (Warner Books, 1999).

PartyLite Gifts**

PartyLite Gifts, Inc., 59 Armstrong Road, Plymouth, MA. Tel: 508-830-3100. Fax: 508-732-5818. Web: www.partylite.com.

In 1973, Colonial Candle of Cape Cod (the original company) set up PartyLite Gifts, Inc. to sell excess inventory of candles from their factory and gift shop in Hyannis, Massachusetts. PartyLite now has more than 37,000 consultants selling candles and candle accessories at home shows. Consultants earn between 25–32%, based on sales, plus a 7% commission on team members. Candles are sold only through home demonstrations. The starter kit is free, and includes candles and accessories, literature, manual, show video, and catalogs. Incentives change from month to month, and include cash, product, and business tools.

Passion Parties**

Passion Parties, 440 Valley Drive, Brisbane, CA 94005. Tel: 800-4PASSION or 415-656-2161. Fax: 415-656-2164. Web: www.passionparties.com.

Passion Parties, formerly Coming Attractions Parties, Inc., was founded in 1994 to sell fun, tasteful, adult toys, sexual aids, and lingerie. They consider their approach educational, and their consultants are trained in enhancing a couple's sex life through the introduction and use of sensual products. Their Director of Professional Education and Communication, Dr. Louanne Cole-Weston, is an expert in human sexuality and helps their consultants increase their understanding of sexuality and its role in healthy relationships. The Passion Party, in the privacy of the customer's home along with her close friends, is their method of selling their sensual products in a positive, supportive environment. The parties include thoughtful descriptions of the variety of products and suggestions for use. Incentives for consultants include trips, a car program, and a yearly convention. Consultants earn 40% commission, plus 3–5% on downline sales, and can also earn monthly cash bonuses. Starter kits are available for $100, $250, or $450, and include products, catalogs, order forms, a training video, and a business manual.

Patchwork & Preserves

Patchwork & Preserves, 1210 US 19, Suite 9, Holiday, FL 34691. Tel: 800-957-9232. Fax: 800-738-1025. E-mail: info@patchworkandpreserves.com. Web: www.patchworkandpreserves.com.

Patchwork & Preserves has crafted a product line that captures authentic Amish workmanship and Pennsylvania Dutch foods. Products range from country-style furniture and décor, to handmade quilts, to jellies and relishes. Consultants earn up to 40% commission, as well as up to 15% override commission on recruits. Their home get-togethers are called "Country Samplers." Incentives include products, trips, and the Fast Lane car program. The starting cost is $50, which includes training material, a career guide, invitations, color catalogs, and supplies. Consultants can then design their own kit by purchasing sample products at 40% off. They also offer a pre-selected Country Sampler Kit for $349.

Petra Fashions**

Petra Fashions, 35 Cherry Hill Drive, Danvers, MA 01923-2594. Tel: 800-738-7248 or 978-777-5853. E-mail: petra@petrafashions.com.
Web: www.petrafashions.com.

Petra (pronounced "Paytra") was founded in 1979 by Jonathan and Ingrid Petra Hodges. Petra Fashions specializes in casual and sensual lifestyle apparel and lingerie. Independent Petra Consultants earn 30% commission on sales. New consultants can receive a $600 start-up kit for $1, which includes sample garments, a training video, business cards, a consultant guide, catalogs, and games booklet. Training is provided through monthly branch meetings, annual events, and upline sponsors.

The Picture Perfect Scrapbook Company

Picture Perfect Scrapbook Company, Tel: 503-256-0355.
Web: www.pictureperfectscrapbookco.com.

The Picture Perfect Scrapbook Company is direct-sales scrapbook company located in Portland, Oregon. They launched the company in January, 2003. At Crop 'N' Shops, PPSC Consultants teach scrapbooking techniques and sell supplies. The PPSC Business Builder Kit is $50 and includes more than $100 in product and business supplies, including an album, scrapbook kits, cardstock, accessories, a business binder, a catalog, consultant agreements, and an order form. Consultants receive 20% commission on direct sales with a 5% commission on first level recruits and a 4% commission on second level recruits.

Premier Designs**

Premier Designs, P.O. Box 619220, Dallas, Texas 75261-9220. (1551 Corporate Drive Irving, Texas 75038-2431.) Tel: 800-486-7378 or 972-550-0955. Fax: 972-580-8222. Web: www.premierdesigns.com.

Premier Designs specializes in a line of high fashion jewelry. Premier is in its 19th year of business. The company has 10,000 consultants in the U.S. Premier Designs Jewelers (distributors) earn 50% commission on personal sales, plus a 10% commission on downline sales on the 1st, 2nd, and 3rd levels of recruits. National rallies, including motivation, training and recognition, are available. Jewelers receive a comprehensive training manual and instruction and guidance from field leaders, as well as an array of audio and video training tapes. The starter kit is $395, which includes *The Guide to Effective Master Jewelers Manual*, catalogs, 100 order forms, audio tapes, and all necessary paperwork. The annual fee to remain a consultant is $350.

Princess House**

Princess House, 470 Myles Standish Blvd., Taunton, MA 02780. Tel: 800-622-0039 or 508-823-6800. E-mail: custsvc@princesshouse.com.
Web: www.princesshouse.com.

Princess House is a direct selling company specializing in products for the home, including hand blown and lead crystal, tableware, cookware, bakeware, serveware and collectibles. The company operates a distribution center in Rural Hall, North Carolina and a headquarters in Taunton, Massachusetts. Princess house currently has 15,000 Lifestyle Consultants and Organizers in the U.S. and Puerto Rico. Princess House also has bilingual opportunities, as Spanish-speaking Lifestyle Consultants are their fastest-growing segment of consultants. The company has a bilingual corporate staff and translated tools and materials to support these Lifestyle Consultants in starting and growing their own businesses.

There are six levels of independent Princess House business owners, beginning with Lifestyle Consultant and rising to Field Organizer, their highest level of management. Incentives include trips, regional and national awards and recognition, and product discounts. Lifestyle Consultants are supported by corporate marketing, sales and customer service professionals as well as business tools, materials, and training. Princess House was established in 1963.

Quiet Places For You

Quiet Places For You, 951 South Pine Street, Suite 120, Spartanburg, SC 29302. Fax: 864-591-1839. Web: www.quietplacesforyour.com.

In 1975, Bob and Sylvia Caldwell, owners of a small bedding plant business, developed a line fragrance sachet envelopes. Today, their current company, Quiet Places for You, has grown into a direct selling company marketing "products with a purpose." Quiet Places is "dedicated to providing women the resources and education to create quiet hearts, homes, & minds." Their purpose is to encourage women to take time out for themselves. To this end, their products fall into three categories. Products to sooth the heart include devotional books and journals for prayer or daily thoughts. Products to decorate the home include home accessories. And products to sooth the mind include bubble baths, lotions, relaxation music, and fragrance products.

There are a few starter kits to choose from. Their Divin' In Starter Kit is $199.00 and contains more than $600 worth of merchandise, including a Fragrance Sampler (one 8-oz. votive jar candle in every fragrance), an assortment of accessories, plus the Deluxe Business Tool Kit with a training DVD, 25 hostess packets, 25 consultant packets, 50 catalogs, 100 order forms, 100 business, and 160 invitations. The Easin' In Starter Kit is $99 contains more than $300 worth of merchandise, including the Fragrance Sampler and a smaller Business Tool Kit (training DVD, 50 catalogs, 100 order forms and 160 invitations).

Consultants earn 25% of personal retail party sales, plus additional percentages on personal sales volume and on the party sales of recruits. There are six levels of management levels attainable, from Consultant to Team Manager.

Richmont Direct**

Richmont Direct, P.O. Box 262529, Plano, Texas 75026. (2400 Dallas Parkway; Suite 230, Plano, Texas 75093.) Tel: 866-312-0800 or 972-309-6000. E-mail: customerservice@richmontdirect.com. Web: www.richmont.net

Founded in 2002, Richmont Direct currently offers four product lines—cooking and entertaining products; Christmas ornaments and décor; jewelry, gifts and collectibles; and Richmont Creations™, a collection of products that can be personalized with a photo or image. Consultants earn up to a 30% commission on all personal sales, and can purchase product samples at a 50% discount. Consultants also earn 6% commission on first-level team members, and an additional 5% commission on the second-level recruits.

Their starter kit is the Success Showcase, which includes sample products from all four product lines (a total of seven items); a three-month, trial subscription to the Richmont Direct Personal Web Page Program; seven catalogs from each product line; a video, "A Conversation with John Rochon," (their founder); literature and forms; the Richmont Consultant Manual; and a silver butterfly pin created by Ross-Simons for new consultants to wear as a conversation-starter for selling and recruiting. The Success Showcase is available for between $74.95–$99, depending on kit special that month (a retail value of $225).

SeneGence International**

SeneGence International, Inc., 4000 Birch Street, Suite 112, Newport Beach, CA 92660. Tel: 949-261-3200. Fax: 949-622-8866. E-mail: info@SeneGence.com. Web: www.senegence.com.

SeneGence International specializes in waterproof cosmetics. Distributors can purchase products at a 20–50% discount can earn 25%+ commission on sales. SeneGence™ Distributors may sell product via in-home or in-office demonstrations, privately-owned non-chain retail establishments, tradeshows, and company-sanctioned Internet and kiosk programs.

They have a variety of start-up options, from $45–$500. The sales packet alone with application deposit is $45 and is refundable upon termination. The New Distributor Kit is $45 (with application deposit waived, but is nonrefundable) and includes the Sales Packet, business supplies, and a training video. The Order Builder Kit is $155, and contains the New Distributor Kit, a product demo video, and business supplies. The SeneCeutical™ Inventory Starter Kit is $500.00 and includes the Complete Starter Kit and pre-selected SeneDerm™ and SeneCosmetic™ inventory for resale. Finally, the Complete Starter Kit is $295 and includes the New Distributor Kit, the Product Demo Kit, the Product Demo Video, and the SeneCeutical™ Product Knowledge CD.

Sensaria**

Sensaria (formerly Natural Bodycare), 3260 East Johns Prairie Road, Suite 1, Shelton, WA 98584-8229. Tel: 360-432-3200. Fax: 360-432-3210. Web: www.sensaria.com.

Sensaria (formerly Natural Bodycare) was founded more than 20 years ago by a chemist who suffered from severe skin allergies due to the chemicals in skin and body care products. Their products are developed using active, natural plant and flower extracts, are safe for the environment, and are not tested on animals. Products include cleansers; moisturizers; basic skin care systems; and sun care products.

Incentives include vacations, investment accounts, and new car payments. No inventory or delivery is required. Training is provided through sponsors, videos, newsletters, training materials, and conference calls. The $115 Natural Start Kit includes a variety of full size products to start doing Sensaria Spa Classes (Retail value: $377). The Business Kit includes samples, catalogs, order forms, Web site, e-mail address, online tools, training DVD, training CDs, and Training manual. Consultants earn 30% commission, plus 5–12% on downline sales.

Shaklee Corporation

Shaklee Corporation, 4747 Willow Road, Pleasanton, CA 94588. Tel: 800-SHAKLEE or 925-924-2000. Fax: 925-924-2862. Web: www.shaklee.com.

Shaklee Corporation is an eight-year-old company that specializes in nutrition, personal, and home care products, including sports and fitness; vitamins and minerals; herbal formulas; personal care and cosmetics; home care products; and air and water purification products. Shaklee Independent Distributors earn 51% commission on sales, plus 5% on team members.

A Shaklee Membership is $19.95 per year, and includes the Shaklee New Member Kit, eligibility for a 15% discount on Shaklee products, and access to special member-only promotions. The Shaklee New Member Kit includes product samples, the 75 page, Shaklee Product Guide, a product videotape, a one-year subscription to the new *Shaklee* catalog, and a personalized Shaklee Member ID card.

Silpada Designs Jewelry

Silpada Designs Jewelry, 16041 Marty Circle, Stilwell, Kansas 66085. Tel: 888-745-7232. Web: www.mysilpada.com.

Bonnie Kelly and Teresa Walsh began selling their sterling silver jewelry at jewelry parties in 1991. In 1997, Bonnie and Teresa expanded the business and Silpada Designs was born. A catalog was created, and long-time customers were invited to become the first independent Silpada Designs Representatives. Today, Silpada Designs is one of the fastest growing direct selling companies in the United States. The company has nearly 3,500 independent sales representatives, a team of more than 130 staff members and professional managers, and a new corporate headquarters in Stilwell, Kansas.

The basic starter kit is $199 and includes catalogs, order forms, recruiting and hostess flyers, invitations, and a consultant manual. Larger kits for $850, and $1,500 include to same business materials, plus a selection of display jewelry. Reps earn 30% profit on each sale, and can earn up to $3,000 in free jewelry during their first 90 days. Other incentives include quarterly and annual contests, and additional training is available through an annual conference.

Simply Satisfying Soaps

Simply Satisfying Soaps, 7719 W. Hunterhill St., Dunnellon, FL., 34433. Tel: 352-564-1406. E-mail: simplysatisfyingsoaps@yahoo.com.
Web: www.simplysatisfyingsoaps.com.

Simply Satisfying Soaps offers glycerin, castile soaps, bath and body products, and candles and gifts. Independent Distributors can purchase products at a 30% discount and may set their own retail prices. The starter kit is $21.95 and contains brochures, order forms, distributor information, the distributor agreement, product details, full-size and sample-size products. Distributors can sell at home parties, flea markets, bazaars, crafts shows, or online.

Southern Living at HOME**

Southern Living at HOME, P.O. Box 830951, Birmingham, AL 35283. Tel: 512-703-8030. E-mail: info@southernlivingathome.com.
Web: www.southernlivingathome.com.

Southern Living at HOME sells home décor and garden items, cooking, garden and idea books, kitchen tools, and food mixes and is connected to the magazine, *Southern Living*. At the end of 2003, there were 31,500 consultants in U.S. The starter kit is $199, which includes $450 worth of product, a supply of catalogs, order forms, consultant manual, and a one-year subscription to *Southern Living* magazine. Consultants earn 25% commission, plus 208$ overrides on team members. Training is provided through an annual conventions and regional trainings.

Southern Living At HOME is the direct sales company of Southern Progress Corporation, a subsidiary of Time Inc. The corporate headquarters are located in Birmingham, Alabama. The company was founded in January 2001.

Stampin' Up!**

Stampin' Up!, 9350 South 150 East, Fifth Floor, Sandy UT 84070. (in 2005, new address will be: 12695 South 3600 West, Riverton, UT 84065). Tel: 800-STAMPUP. Fax: 801-601-5445. E-mail: ds@stampinup.com. Web: www.stampinup.com.

Stampin' Up! sells wood-mounted decorative rubber stamps and accessories for use in creating greeting cards and scrapbook pages, as well as home décor and other craft projects. The stamps are sold at home workshops in the U.S. and Canada through a network of nearly 40,000 Demonstrators. Demonstrators earn 20% commission on sales, plus up to an additional 12% based on monthly sales. Downline commissions are between 2–5%. The company has been in business for 16 years.

The standard starter kit is $199 (a retail value of $360), and includes a sampling of rubber stamps, assorted ink pads, card stock, accessories, the Demonstrator Manual, the current catalog, introductory videos, getting started information, stampin' techniques brochure, and order forms and business supplies. Larger starter kits are available for $249.

The Story Teller

The Story Teller, P.O. Box 921, 308 E. 800 S., Salem, UT 84653. Tel: 800-801-6860. Fax: 801-423-2568. Web: www.thestoryteller.com.

The Story Teller sells felt boards and puppets with audio tapes and books for use in telling stories to children. The starter kit is $100 (a retail value of $235), and includes a selection of felt products and audio tapes, the consultant training manual, a training video, an order book, order forms, consultant applications, catalogs, mini-catalogs, flyers, invitations, scissors, briefcase, and thank-you gifts. The Mini-Supply Kit is $30 and contains business supplies only. Training is provided through the consultant section of their Web site, the manual, and the training tapes. The company also has a newsletter, area training meetings, and a national convention. Reps earn up to 35% commission on sales, plus 1–15% on team member sales. Incentives include trips and monthly promotions.

Sweet Berry Fields

Sweet Berry Fields, 5585 Bethlehem Road, Mulberry, Florida 33860. Tel: 941-313-0643. E-mail: sweetberryfields@aol.com. Web: www.sweetberryfields.com.

Sweet Berry Fields was founded in 2003 and specializes in gourmet foods, homemade candles, and soaps, as well as hand-carved wooden shadowboxes. Reps earn 30% commission on sales, up to 35% based on total party order. Managers earn 8–10% on sales aides, and can earn free product by building a team. There are 5 levels of SBF management. The basic "I'll Give it a Try" Kit is $9.99 and the "I'm Just Gonna Do It" kit is $49.99. The company also offers an SBF redirect Web site with a $44.95 setup fee ($29.95 renewed annually.).

Taste of Gourmet

Taste of Gourmet, P.O. Box 540, 36 Sunflower Rd, Indianola, MS 38751. Tel: 800-722-8931 or 662-887-2522. Fax: 662-887-5547. Web: www.tasteofgourmet.com.

Taste of Gourmet sells gourmet foods and beverages. They specialize in ready-to-eat appetizers; condiments; main dishes and breads; desserts; beverages; and gourmet gifts. The company offers 60 products for sale through their Independent Gourmet Consultants. Their Sample and Sales Kit Full Kit is $195 (a retail value of $400) and includes food samples for more than 20 tastings, the Training Manual, and business supplies for at least 6 tastings (catalogs, interview booklets, invitations, tote bag, apron, tablecloth, customer care cards, condiment cups, cookbooks, hostess packets, and a training CD and video). The Mini Sample and Sales Kit is $75 (a retail value of $135) and contains product samples for 8 to 10 Tastings and business supplies for at least 6 tastings. Consultants earn 25–30% commission on sales, plus 1–4% on downline sales.

Taste of Home Parties

Taste of Home Parties, 1680 Hwy 1 North, Fairfield IA 52556.
E-mail: demonstrator@tasteofhomeparties.com.
Web: www.tasteofhomeparties.com.

In 1993, Reiman Publications launched *Taste of Home*, an ad-free magazine featuring home-style recipes submitted by its readers. When Reiman Publications was purchased by The Reader's Digest Association, Inc. in 2002, doors opened for new business ventures between Reiman Publications and its sister RDA companies, such as Books Are Fun, Ltd. Books Are Fun is the world's leading display marketer of books and gifts. Reiman Publications and Books Are Fun have now joined resources to create Taste of Home Parties. Through independent Demonstrators and a direct sales party plan, Taste of Home Parties sell cookbooks, kitchenwares, home accessories, and gifts.

Taste of Home Parties Demonstrators receive a 25% commission on sales, a 50% discount on products, and special incentives for reaching sales or recruiting goals. They also earn 4% commission on downline sales. The basic starter kit is $149, which includes an assortment of top-selling products and business forms.

Tastefully Simple

Tastefully Simple, 1920 Turning Leaf Lane SW, P.O. Box 3006, Alexandria, MN 56308-3006. Tel: 320-763-0695. Fax: 320-763-2458. Referrals Line: 866-328-6673. Web: www.tastefullysimple.com.

Tastefully Simple was founded in Alexandria, Minnesota in June of 1995, and now sells more than 30 easy-to-prepare gourmet foods through home tasting parties. Training and support include The Business Blast Off Kit; team support at headquarters; the Gourmet Gazette (newsletter); Gourmet Gab (monthly publications) all-consultant emails; and online office for consultants; and national, regional, and leadership conferences. Incentives include trips, jewelry, Spiegel products, and cash bonuses. Tastefully Simple offers commissions ranging from 20–36%. Downline commissions are 5% on first line recruits, 3% on second line recruits, and 1% on third line recruits. The Business Blast Off Kit is $170 (often on special for $99) and includes $700 worth of retail products and paperwork for six parties.

Top Line Creations**

Top Line Creations, 3759 West 2340 South, Suite D, SLC, Utah 84120. Tel: 866-954-0559 or 801-954-0559. Fax: 801-954-0370.
Email: info@topline-creations.com. Web: www.topline-creations.com.

Top Line Creations (TLC) sells scrapbooking supplies such as post-bound, top loading albums, 3-ring binder albums, album refills, adhesives, page kits, tags, mini tags, letter stickers, die cuts, mini frames, vellum, phrase stickers, and more. The company has been in business approximately 2 years as Top Line Creations (previously it was known as Cock-a-Doodle Designs). There are approximately 3,000 consultants in the U.S. and Canada.

TLC consultants earn 25–45% commission on sales, plus 5–10% on downline sales. The starter kit is $100 and includes one Total LapTop Crop Bag, catalogs, marketing folders, six page element kits, order forms, applications and agreements, three collective elements bags, two 12x12 storyline pages, two 4x6 lifeline cards, two 50% coupons, and a consultant CD.

The Traveling Vineyard**

The Traveling Vineyard, 960 Turnpike Street, Canton, MA 02021. Tel: 866-547-9463. Fax: 800-329-8466. E-mail: info@thetravelingvineyard.com. Web: www.thetravelingvineyard.com.

The Traveling Vineyard was designed with the belief that the best way to buy wine is to taste it first. They offer in-home wine tasting parties through Personal Wine Consultants. Their first event, run as they are today, occurred in April of 2002 under the name Taste D'Vine. By that time they had five consultants in three states. At of the end of 2002, they had grown to more than 50 Consultants in 7 states. The company was renamed The Traveling Vineyard in June of 2003. Prior wine expertise is not required. The Traveling Vineyard provides all of the training to become a Personal Wine Consultant. Their Starter Kit is $250 and includes more than $400 worth of materials, including a training manual, and a wine course book, a video to help you learn about their products and the process, and accessories for use at tastings. Bi-weekly training sessions and monthly meetings are available. As new wines are bottled, Team Leaders hold Tasting Sessions to give consultants a chance to taste the new wines. Wine consultants earn 20% on sales, plus 2–5% on team members.

Tupperware**

Tupperware Corporation, P.O. Box 2353, Orlando, FL 32802. Tel: 800-366-3800. Web: http://my.tupperware.com.

Tupperware has been in business for 54 years. They sell kitchen products and gadgets, most well-known for their invention of the self-sealing "burp" of the plastic Tupperware container. Consultants sell mainly through home parties, and earn between 25–35% commission on sales. Commissions on team members range from 3–5%. The starter kit includes $100 worth of products and approximately $25 in business supplies, all of which costs $63.

Two Sisters Gourmet

Two Sisters Gourmet, 28312 Hayes Road, Roseville, MI 48066. Tel: 586-777-7070. Fax: 586-777-5105. E-mail: info@twosistersgourmet.com. Web: www.twosistersgourmet.com.

Two Sisters Gourmet was created by Lori Caruso and Catherine Hackenberger, sisters-in-law, to help people get involved in the gourmet cooking experience. Two Sisters Gourmet is a 4-year-old company and has more than 150 consultants across the U.S. The sisters travel throughout the United States to search for new gourmet product trends and ideas. They pride their products as simple to prepare, offer gourmet tastes, enhance the ordinary, and have multiple uses. A sampling of products include: raspberry grilling & dipping sauce; beer bread; black bean and corn salsa; peanut ginger marinade; porcini mushroom balsmaic dressing; mango salsa with peach; creamy wild rice soup; apple cake; and cranberry scones.

Consultants sell Two Sisters Gourmet products through Home Tasting Parties and on the Internet, and can also branch out into craft shows, fundraisers, gift baskets, corporate business, and holiday bazaars. The Welcome Kit is $99 (a retail value of $175) and includes the Gourmet Consultant Manual; product samples from core items; tasting party presentation script cards; 3 hostess kits; 100 invitations; 100 order forms; 100 product menus; fliers; party recap forms; planning your party brochures; career opportunity brochures; and a divided serving tray.

Consultants earn 25% on all orders. Downline commissions vary by the level of management achieved, from 3–7%. Incentives include leadership awards, service awards; incentive trips, consultant appreciation program; yearly convention; and personal bonuses.

UBB's Natural Family Boutique**

Unique Natural Family Boutique, 17232 Pickwick Drive, Purcellville, VA 20132-3100. Tel: 866-672-7843 or 540-338-0330. Fax: 703-783-0511E-mail: webmaster@uniquebabyboutique.com. Web: www.uniquebabyboutique.com.

Unique Baby Boutique was founded in 2002 by Kim Pekin, a breastfeeding advocate and mother committed to attachment parenting. Her company is dedicated to providing attachment parenting, breastfeeding, and natural childbirth products. Product categories include pregnancy; labor and birth; postpartum; breastfeeding; mommy pampering; natural baby care; cloth diapering; organic baby clothing; wooden toys; non-toxic art products; baby slings; natural birth and parenting books and videos; belly casting/hand and foot casting kits; organic bedding; beeswax candles; Holly Lane Designs Jewelry, and more. UBB Sales Consultants earn 25% commission on sales, plus 2–3% on team members. Commission can rise as high as 40% with downline sales and bonuses. The UBB Mini Kit is $99 (a retail value of more than $165) and contains 6 product samples, catalogs, order forms, and binder. The UBB Basic Kit is $249 (a retail value of more than $400) and contains 13 best-selling products, business supplies, catalogs, brochures, invitations, business cards, fabric swatches, hostess packet, recruit packet, order forms, and binder. There is also a Doula Business Start-Up Kit for $169 (retail value of $500) and containing 10 natural childbirth products samples, business supplies, catalogs, order forms, and binder. With a 50% down payment, consultants can pay for the starter kits over a two-month period.

USANA Health Sciences**

USANA Health Sciences, 3838 West Parkway Blvd., Salt Lake City, UT 84120. Tel: 801-954-7200. Fax: 801-954-7300. E-mail: distserv@usana.com. Web: www.usana.com.

USANA offers health products, including Usana Essentials (vitamins), Optimizers (nutritional products), and Macro-Optimizers (macro-nutrients). Independent Associate commissions vary based on a complex multi-level recruit system. Starter kits range from $250 to $1,250 and contain a variety of products, training materials, and marketing materials, depending on the kit purchased. Training is available online, through conference calls, regional and national conferences, and conventions. Reps earn between 10–20% commission on sales, plus 10–20% on downline sales.

Usborne Books at Home**

Usborne Books at Home, A Division of Educational Development Corporation, 10302 E. 55th Place, Tulsa, OK 74146-6515. Tel: 800-475-4522. Fax: 800-747-4509. E-mail: edc@edcpub.com or ubah@ubah.com. Web: www.ubah.com

Usborne Books at Home (UBAH) is the home business division of Educational Development Corporation (EDC). EDC began this home business division in March 1989, and was the first multilevel direct selling company in the United States to offer primarily nonfiction educational books for children. Usborne Books at Home markets the entire Usborne line of more than 1,000 titles through a combination of direct sales, home parties, fundraisers, and book fairs. Their independent sales consultants are selling books in all 50 states and number approximately 5,700.

The Base Kit is $199 and includes approximately 30 books, as well as a selection of catalogs, order forms, customer surveys, flyers and the UBAH Handbook. Special kits are available and change every two months. Consultants earn 25% commission on home show sales, and 17–25% on book fairs and school and library sales. Downline commissions range from 1–11%. Incentives include recruiting bonuses, sales bonuses, and contests.

Villa Beautiful

Villa Beautiful, 1401 N. Pruett, Baytown, TX 77520. Tel: 281-422-9300. Fax: 281-420-7631. E-mail: info@villabeautiful.com. Web: www.villabeautiful.com

Villa Beautiful was founded by David G. Balzen and Callie Woodward in 2002 to sell home and garden décor. The products range from attractive wall hangings and candles to wind chimes and plant stakes, as well as a selection of gourmet foods (butterscotch apple-streusel muffins and cheesy jalapeno bread, to name two). Consultants earn 25% commissions on sales, plus a 5% bonus on referral sales from sponsored consultants. "The Villa" Kit includes a sample of products, catalogs, order forms, a training guide, and invitations and costs $199 (a $500 value). Incentives include trips and prizes.

VitaCorp International**

Vitacorp International, 13100 Northwest Fwy, Suite 440, Houston, TX 77040. Tel: 281-220-1240. Fax: 832-201-7517. E-mail: questions@vitacorp.com. Web: www.vitacorp.com.

Vitacorp offers a line of vitamins, minerals, herbals, botanicals, enzymes and homeopathics. The cost for enrolling as an affiliate is $29, which includes a personalized Web site, group management tools, web-based resources, and twelve months of business support. The annual renewal fee of $10 is waived for affiliates who have earned at least $100 in bonuses during the previous calendar year.

Warm Spirit**

Warm Spirit, Inc., Field Services Department, 15645 SE 114th Avenue, Suite 202, Clackamas, OR 97015. Tel: 888-296-9854. E-mail: fieldsupport@warmspirit.com. Web: www.warmspirit.com.

Warm Spirit sells a line of bath and body products, including: Essentials (soaps, cleansers, toners; creams, balms, lotions; healthy hair; masks and body treatments; vitamins and supplements); Pleasures (body butters; massage, body and bath; gift pillows and sachets; therapeutic pillows; and herbal teas); Remedies (homeopathic formulas and herbal remedies to ease things from backache to PMS to diet support to sore throat.).

The Basic Kit is $99 and includes product samples, literature and business tools, and paperwork (a retail value of $175). Optional product kits to add on to your basic kit are available, ranging from $200–$500. Consultants earn 25% personal sales commission. Consultants earn gift certificates for new recruits.

Watkins International

Watkins International, 150 Liberty Street, P.O. Box 5570, Winona, MN 55987-0570. Tel: 800-243-9423 or 507-457-3300. Fax: 507-452-6723. Web: www.watkinsonline.com.

Watkins International began in 1868 when 28-year-old J.R. Watkins founded the J.R. Watkins Medical Company in Plainview, Minnesota to sell natural remedies. Today, Watkins International sells gourmet foods, herbal personal care products and medicinals, dietary supplements, and cleaning products with earth-friendly ingredients and biodegradable formulas. Independent Associates earn 19% commission from sales, and can earn additional bonus income based on their personal sales and the sales team members. Starter kits range from $49.95 to $399.99 and include training materials, a sampling of Watkins products. Incentives include trips and recognition awards.

Weekenders USA

Weekenders USA, Vernon Hills, IL. Web: www.weekendersusa.com.

Weekenders USA has been in business for 14 years selling women's clothing through home parties. The company has consultants in six countries. Consultants earn 40% commission on sales, with between 1 and 15% earned on team members. The cost to start depends on the size of pack in the starter kit, ranging from 0 (no pack) to $1,500. The starter kit includes one of every item being sold that season, plus all paperwork needed. Weekenders USA consultants mainly sell through home parties. Sales incentives and bonuses include jewelry, trips, and bonus commission.

Weekenders USA is headquartered in Vernon Hills, Illinois. Rosemary Redmond, President, started the company in 1988 with just a handful of Fashion Coordinators. Today the company has close to 16,000 Fashion Coordinators nationwide.

Wildtree Herbs**

Wildtree Herbs, Inc., 11 Knight Street, Warwick, Rhode Island 02886. Tel: 800-672-4050 or 401-732-1856. Fax: 401-732-1968.
E-mail: repinfo@wildtreeherbs.com. Web: www.wildtreeherbs.com.

Wildtree Herbs Inc. is a new direct-sales company offering gourmet culinary blends, infused oils, dressings, and sauces sold through home parties. Their Independent Representatives show how to make cooking a quicker, easier, and more healthful project for those who are short on time. Wildtree Herbs was established as a small craft/hobby business several years ago by Leslie Montie. Today, Wildtree Herbs products are free of preservatives, added MSG, fillers, and anti-caking agents. Reps earn 25% commission on sales, plus 3–15% on team member bonuses. The starter kit is $100 and includes business supplies, training materials, bulk products, top-selling oils, dips, seasonings, and sauces. Starter kit enhancements are available, and the kit can be earned for free.

Woods Potpourri

Wood's Potpourri, 311 Ashton St., New Iberia, LA 70563. Tel: 337-364-4781.
Email: info@woodspotpourri.com. Web: www.woodspotpourri.com.

Wood's Potpourri offers potpourri, candles, and bath and body products. Consultants earn 25% commission on sales. There are several starter kits to choose from. The kits range from $9.99–$40, each containing a selection of products and business paperwork.

zeBlooms

zeBlooms, Inc., 8200 Marshall Drive, Lenexa, KS 66214. Tel: 913-599-2199. Fax: 913-599-2399. E-mail: advisorservices@zeblooms.com. Web: www.zeblooms.com.

zeBlooms is a home party plan company that provides customers home decorating ideas with a floral focus. The company has been in business since August 2002, and has approximately 150 consultants in the U.S. zeBlooms Advisors receive a personal sponsor; online business support and training tools; national training at zeBlooms' annual Flower Show; regular promotions with rewards and recognition; and travel incentives. The Advisor Sample Kit is $149.99 and includes décor products, floral arrangements, sample containers, catalogs, order forms, and business enhancers (a retail value of more than $450). Training is provided through an advisor Web site, monthly newsletters, weekly training calls, an annual National Flower Show, the Advisor Manual, a home show video, and upline sponsors. Advisors earn 25% commission on sales, plus a 5% personal bonus based on sales volume. There is also 2–10% commission on the sales of team members.

Zedora, Inc.**

Zedora, Inc. (formerly Manuel.Zed) 110 East Broward Blvd., Suite 1910, Fort Lauderdale, FL 33301. Tel: 954-332-3322. Fax: 954-332-0028. Web: www.zedora.com.

Zedora Inc. specializes in a collection of Italian charms for bracelets is inspired by artisan Manuel Zoppini's passion for detailed design, style, and a desire to "merge classical fashion with contemporary expression." The Manuel.Zed bracelets are made up of interlocking charms made of stainless steel in a wide variety of images. Since their name change from Manuel.Zed to Zedora, the company has now broadened their product selection to carry a variety of jewelry pieces and leather accessories. Consultants earn 35% commission on sales, plus 2% on team members through four levels, as well as infinity bonuses. The starter kit is $99 and includes business cards, brochures, a training manual, and consultant packets. Larger kits with jewelry cost up to $2,000.

At-a-Glance Company Profiles

This section includes profiles with contact information from the following companies:

Affordable Luxuries
Arbonne International
AtHome America, Inc.
BeautiControl, Inc.
The Bittersweet Candle Company
Cell Tech
Country Bunny Bath and Body
Demarle at Home
Discovery Toys, Inc.
Enchanting Scents Designs
FemOne
For Your Pleasure, Inc.
The Fuller Brush Company
Gabby Goodies
Gifted Expressions
Herbalife International, Inc.
Home and Garden Party
The Homemaker's Idea Company
HomeWare Creations
Joielle Fine Jewelry
Mary Kay Cosmetics
My Precious Kid
Northern Lights at Home
Nouveau Cosmeceuticals
Nu Skin International
Once Upon a Charm…®
Once Upon a Family
PartyLite Gifts
Passion Parties
Petra Fashions
Premier Designs Jewelry
Princess House
Richmont Direct
SeneGence International
Sensaria
Southern Living at HOME

Stampin' Up!

Top Line Creations

The Traveling Vineyard

Tupperware

UBB's Natural Family Boutique

USANA Health Sciences

Usborne Books at Home

VitaCorp International

Warm Spirit

Wildtree Herbs, Inc.

Zedora, Inc.

Affordable Luxuries

Affordable Luxuries specializes in scented candles. They craft their own collection of candles in a small chandlery in rural Massachusetts, using a premium soft jelly/paraffin wax blend. The candles come in travel tins or votives, or in their exclusive AL Jars, durable curved-glass vases. They also offer Yankee Candles and root candles (soy). AL's Business Starter Kit costs $25 and provides more than $85 in educational materials, sales tools, and a supply of catalogs. Also included is an AL myWebStore subscription. AL's Home Demonstration Kit costs $199. The Home Demonstration Kit is worth more than $400 and contains all the materials to hold a full-featured "Candle Experience" (their home show and demonstration). The Home Demonstration Kit includes a wide assortment of AL candle and accessory products, educational materials, sales tools, a supply of catalogs, as well as the AL myWebStore subscription. Consultants earn 25–40% commission on sales with 6% on team members, plus 5–8% monthly sales bonuses.

Company: Affordable Luxuries, 569 High Street, Westwood, MA 02090. Tel: 781-326-6800. Fax: 617-663-6007. E-mail: info@affordableluxuries.us. Web: www.affordableluxuries.us.

Products: Candles and accessories

Years in Business: 2 years

Countries of Operation: U.S. and Canada

Starter Kit/Start-Up Costs: Business Starter Kit is $25 (worth $85) and contains educational tools, sales tools, and catalogs. Home Demonstration Kit is $199 (worth $400) and contains the same materials as the Starter Kit, adding a candle assortment.

Annual Fee to Remain a Consultant: None

Sales Method: Home Shows ("Candle Experiences")

Training: Business Building Manual, along with sponsor training

Online Shop Available? Yes

Commissions: 25–40% commission on sales

Downline Structure: 6% commission on recruits

Incentives and Bonuses: 5–8% monthly sales bonuses

Inventory: No

Territories: No

Quotas: No quota to remain active, but must sell $275 a month to receive downline commissions.

Member of DSA? No

Contact a Representative in Your Area!

COLORADO

Angela Thurlow, Team Director, Aurora, CO. Tel: (720) 870-3536. E-mail: amthurlow@comcast.net. Web: www.shopaffordableluxuries.us/athurlow.

FLORIDA

Ruth Carter, Founding Independent Consultant, FL. Tel: (772) 567-4929. Fax: 772-567-3140. E-mail: RCarter9735@aol.com.
Web: www.shopaffordableluxuries.us/rcarter.

ILLINOIS

Laura Mensching, Team Director/Independent Consultant, Des Plaines, IL. Tel: (847) 299-0673. E-mail: slmensching@comcast.net.
Web: www.premiumcandles.us.

MICHIGAN

Jackie Bolhuis, Zeeland, MI. Tel: (616) 875-3011. E-mail: jbolhuis@chartermi.net. Web: www.shopaffordableluxuries.us/JackieBolhuis.

MISSOURI

Charles Gray, Kansas City, MO. Tel: (816) 547-7492.
E-mail: charlesgray@acninc.net. Web: www.shopaffordableluxuries.us/grayarea.

NEW YORK

Yvonne Cruz, Founding Consultant, Kew Gardens Hills, NY. Tel: (718) 380-1723. E-mail: yvonne@affordableluxuries.us. Web: www.shopaffordableluxuries.us/ycruz.

TEXAS

Dee Diane Smith, Independent Candle Consultant, Dallas, TX. Tel: (972) 248-6407. Fax: 972-248-4327. E-mail: Dee.Smith@AffordableLuxuries.us. Web: www.shopaffordableluxuries.us/deesmith.

Arbonne International

Arbonne International sells Swiss skin care products based on botanical principles, and became a reality in the United States in 1980. Arbonne's product line has since grown to include both inner and outer health and beauty products. Independent Consultants earn 35% commission and can earn cash bonuses and 4% commission overrides. Arbonne offers the choice of two Starter Kits, the Quick Start Kit for $29 and the Super Start for $65. The company also has a fax-on-demand system from which you can automatically receive the consultant agreement (call 949-455-1004 and request document #520). Incentives include trips, cash bonuses, and a Mercedes-Benz car program.

Company: Arbonne International, Inc., 4 Cromwell, Irvine, CA 92618. Tel: 949-770-2610 or 800-272-6663. Fax: (949) 837-8415.
E-mail: customerservice@arbonne.com. Web: www.arbonne.com.

Products: Botanical skin care products

Years in Business: Since 1980.

Countries of Operation: U.S. and Canada with licensees/global sponsoring in Iceland, Korea, Mexico, Venezuela, and Sweden.

Starter Kit/Start-Up Costs: Quick Start Kit is $29 and includes the consultant manual, catalog, SuccessPlan summary, retail price list and order form, consultant application, autoship program agreement, Fitness® for Men Sample Pack, Normal/Dry Sample Pack, Discover Arbonne audio tape and Arbonne Folder. The SuperStart Kit is $69 and includes consultant manual, scheduling calendar, 3 product catalogs, consultant applications, order forms, 3 autoship program agreements, Discover Arbonne audio tape, presentation flipchart, hostess brochures, invitations, product knowledge manual, product knowledge audio, Arbonne Starter Kit bag, and Arbonne Sample Packs—Normal/Dry Sample Pack, Normal/Oily Sample Pack, and Arbonne Skin Fitness® for Men Sample Pack.

Annual Fee to Remain a Consultant: $15

Sales Method: Home parties, direct selling

Training: National conference, local and regional meetings, weekly teleconference calls, audio and video training

Online Shop Available? Yes

Commissions: 35% commission on sales

Downline Structure: 4% on approved recruits

Incentives and Bonuses: Cash bonuses, Mercedes-Benz car program, trips.

Inventory: No

Territories: No

Quotas: Must sell $100 a month to remain active. Other quotas apply for higher levels to receive overrides.

Member of DSA? Yes

Contact a Representative in Your Area!

ALABAMA

Jennifer Dormany, District Manager, Pensacola, FL. Tel: (850) 712-8691. E-mail: jennifer@atotalu.com. Web: www.atotalu.com.

ARIZONA

Jennifer Welborn, Consultant, Surprise, AZ. Tel: (623) 826-3845. E-mail: welborn99@aol.com. Web: www.arbonne.com ID#10510054.

CALIFORNIA

Jennifer Dormany, District Manager, Pensacola, FL. Tel: (850) 712-8691. E-mail: jennifer@atotalu.com. Web: www.atotalu.com.

COLORADO

Jennifer Dormany, District Manager, Pensacola, FL. Tel: (850) 712-8691. E-mail: jennifer@atotalu.com. Web: www.atotalu.com.

FLORIDA

Jennifer Dormany, District Manager, Pensacola, FL. Tel: (850) 712-8691. E-mail: jennifer@atotalu.com. Web: www.atotalu.com.

ILLINOIS

Gwen Wolken, Area Manager, Independent Consultant, Northbrook, IL. Tel: (847) 559-9564. Fax: (847) 559-9557. E-mail: Gwen@myarbonne.com. Web: www.Gwen.arbonne.com.

MICHIGAN

Barbara Galster, Shelby Twp., MI. Tel: (586) 739-3857.
E-mail: bgalster@hotmail.com

OHIO

Kathy Whittington, Independent Executive Regional Vice President, Pickerington, OH. Toll-free: (888) 293-6185. Tel: (614) 833-2366. Fax: (614) 837-2760. E-mail: kathy@ascendingwings.com. Web: www.ascendingwings.com.

VIRGINIA

Cathy Peterson, Independent Consultant, Sterling, VA. Tel: (703) 404-2893.E-mail: cathypeterson@myarbonne.com. Web: www.visit.myarbonne.com.

AtHome America, Inc.

AtHome America specializes in home products, including home décor, homewares, baskets, bedding, furniture, dinnerware, and candles. The company was founded in 1982 by co-founders and sisters Lisa Brandau and Becky Wright, who still hand-pick each product they sell. Their HomeStyle Specialists earn up to 30% commission and receive discounts up to 50% on personal orders, plus 2–12% commission on downline sales. The starter kit includes catalogs, home show invitations, order forms, promotional flyers, a training guide, training materials on video and audio cassettes, and a searchable CD-ROM and costs $149 (a $600 value).

The company has nearly 10,000 HomeStyle Specialists in the U.S. Incentives include product discounts, charms, trips, and prizes. Extra training is available through local and nationwide training conferences.

Company: AtHome America, Inc., 5625 West 115th Street, Alsip, IL 60803. Tel: 800-928-4663 or 708-597-1085. Fax: 708-597-1435. Web: www.athome.com.

Products: Home décor, housewares, baskets, bedding, furniture, dinnerware, and candles

Years in Business: Since 1983

Countries of Operation: U.S.

Starter Kit/Start-Up Costs: Starter kit contains catalogs, invitations, order forms, flyers, a training guide, video and audio training, and searchable CD-ROM, and costs $149 (a retail value of $600).

Sales Method: Home shows

Training: Training guide, and video and audio training included in starter kit. Local and nationwide training conferences available.

Online Shop Available? Yes

Commissions: 20–30% commission on sales. On personal orders consultants receive a 50% discount.

Downline Structure: 2–12% commission on downline sales

Incentives and Bonuses: Product discounts, charms, trips, and prizes

Inventory: No

Territories: No

Quotas: Must sell $1,000 per month to receive override commissions

Company Accolades: Ernst & Young's Women Entrepreneurs of the Year; Inc. 500

Member of DSA? Yes

Contact a Representative in Your Area!

ARIZONA

Luree Harrington, HomeStyle Specialist, Glendale, AZ. Tel: (623) 334-3917. Fax: (623) 334-3917. E-mail: athomewithluree@aol.com.
Web: www.athome.com/luree.

CALIFORNIA

Laurie Swindell, HomeStyle Specialist, Alsip, CA. Tel: (510) 278-0358. Fax: (510) 278-7860. E-mail: lauriesll@aol.com. Web: www.athomeamerica.com/LaurieSwindell.

DELAWARE

Michelle Torbert, Delaware. E-mail: Torbert63@msn.com.

ILLINOIS

Kim Hughes, Homestyle Specialist 3 Star Team Leader, Illinois. Tel: (217) 497-8485. E-mail: kimsathome4u@hotmail.com. Web: www.athome.com/hughes.

INDIANA

Joyce Ransom, Bronze Star Executive, Williamsport, IN. Tel: (765) 762-2187. Fax: (765) 762-2187. E-mail: joyceraha@aol.com. Web: www.athome.com/joyceransom.

KENTUCKY

Kim Woods, Ohio. Toll-free: (888) 243-9647. E-mail: pdlnfool@aol.com. Web: www.athome.com/KimWoods.

MISSOURI

Lori Smith, Silver Star Executive, Jefferson City, MO. Tel: (573) 761-3515. Fax: (573) 761-3515. E-mail: ranlor90@hotmail.com.
Web: www.athome.com/LoriSmith.

NEW YORK

Tammy Russell, Gold Star Executive, Medina, NY. Tel: (585) 798-9167. Fax: (585) 798-2950. E-mail: TamByGrace@aol.com.
Web: www.athome.com/TammyRussell.

OHIO

Kim Woods, Executive, Groveport, Ohio. Tel: (614) 836-9848. Fax: (614) 836-9819. E-mail: KimWoodsAHA@aol.com. Web: www.athome.com/KimWoods.

PENNSYLVANIA

Jane Mohn, Senior Executive Director, Shillington, PA. Toll-free: (800) 898-7827. Fax: (610) 777-3170. E-mail: JaneMohn@aol.com. www.athome.com/JaneMohn.

RHODE ISLAND

Susan B. Daly, HomeStyle Specialist, Warwick, RI. Tel: (401) 921-2191. E-mail: sdaly3@cox.net. Web: www.athome.com/suedaly.

WASHINGTON

Dawn Dombrowski, HomeStyle Specialist, Puyallup, WA. Tel: (253) 380-1394. Fax: (253) 840-9011. E-mail: dawn.at@netzero.com.
Web: www.athome.com/dawn.

BeautiControl, Inc.

BeautiControl Cosmetics offers skin care, image, and glamour products and has been in business for 20 years. Consultants earn 40–50% commission on sales and 4–12% on team member sales. To remain a consultant, you must sell $100 retail every 4 months. The cost to start is $250, with opportunities to purchase the starter kit for less during specials every month. The starter kit contains products and sales aids, enough for four parties. Bonuses and incentives include trips, jewelry, cash, and more.

More than 50,000 BeautiControl Independent Skin Care and Image Consultants. Founded in 1982, BeautiControl is based in Dallas and is a wholly owned subsidiary of Tupperware Corporation, a $1 billion multinational company and one of the world's leading direct sellers and suppliers of premium food storage, preparation and serving items operating in more than 100 countries. Building on Tupperware's strength in the global marketplace, BeautiControl is rapidly expanding into the large Latin America direct-selling market.

The starter kit is $99–$250 and contains more than $800 worth of beauty products, literature, business-building services and image training. It also includes one day of classroom training (a $200 value); official certification as a professional Independent Skin Care and Image Consultant; their BeautiCase filled with products, tools and literature; a personalized Web page, free for six months (a $60 value); and a free six-month membership in their direct mail program (a $17.50 value).

Company: BeautiControl, Inc., P.O. Box 815189, Dallas, TX 75381-5189. Physical address: 2121 Midway Road, Carrollton, TX 75006. Tel: 800-232-8841. E-mail: clientservices@beauticontrol.com. Web: www.beauticontrol.com.

Products: Skin care, image, and glamour products

Years in Business: More than 20 years

Countries of Operation: U.S., Canada, Puerto Rico

Starter Kit/Start-Up Costs: $99–$250 for BeautiCase, which contains products and sales aides for four parties. Discounted kit specials are available monthly.

Annual Fee to Remain a Consultant: None

Sales Method: Home parties.

Training: Sponsor trainings, monthly meetings and annual conventions, online meetings

Online Shop Available? Yes

Commissions: 40–50% commission on sales

Downline Structure: 4–12% commission on team members

Incentives and Bonuses: Ford Mustang car program, trips, diamond jewelry, on-stage recognition, and in-print recognition in *The Achiever*.

Inventory: Some inventory needed

Territories: No

Quotas: Must sell $100 retail every 4 months to remain active.

Member of DSA? Yes

Contact a Representative in Your Area!

ILLINOIS

Holly Hedlund, National Trainer/Senior Director, Chicago, IL. Tel: (312) 573-9767. E-mail: HhedlundBC@aol.com. Web: www.beautipage.com/hollyhedlund.

KENTUCKY

Ann Ezell, SkinCare, Image, and Spa Specialist, Louisville, KY. Tel: (502) 239-4857. E-mail: annezell@peoplepc.com. Web: www.beautipage.com/skincare.

The Bittersweet Candle Company

The Bittersweet Candle Company is a family owned direct sales company that hand-makes premium candles. They employ a team level marketing concept to distribute their products through independent representatives consisting of primarily at-home moms. The company was started by Gene and Heather Kramer as a project in the basement, and in 2000 their first rep began selling the candles. They plan to branch out into handmade spa products in Fall 2004. Independent reps earn up to 30% commission on retail sales. There are no monthly sales quotas and no shipping and handling fees. Bittersweet Candle has 1,000 sales representatives in the U.S. selling candles and accessories at home parties.

Company: The Bittersweet Candle Company, 5230 Park Emerson Drive, Suite I, Indianapolis, IN 46203. Tel: 317-881-2930. Fax: 317-881-2240. E-mail: sale@bittersweetcandle.com. Web: www.bittersweetcandle.com.

Products: Handmade candle products and accessories. Handmade spa products coming in Fall 2004.

Years in Business: 4½ years

Countries of Operation: U.S.

Starter Kit/Start-Up Costs: $70–$89. Kit includes scent sampler, brochures, invitations, jar candles and retails for $100.

Sales Method: Home parties and direct selling

Training: Regular sales and management training. One on one and group training. Company sponsored training twice a year.

Online Shop Available? Yes

Commissions: 30–40% commission on sales

Downline Structure: 2–10% commission on downline sales

Incentives and Bonuses: Trips, top sales cash bonus, ongoing promotions

Inventory: No

Territories: No

Quotas: No

Company Accolades: Five Star Award from the American Cancer Society for donations from the sale of their "Remembrance" candle.

Member of DSA? Yes

Contact a Representative!

Marilyn Swinford, Senior Team Sales Manager, Indiana. Tel: (765) 525-6284. E-mail: mswinford@bittersweetcandle.com. Web: www.maryilynswaxshack.com.

Cell Tech

Cell Tech's primary product is Super Blue Green® Algae, a super nutritional and a "unique, truly extraordinary food." Cell Tech now harvests millions of pounds of Algae each year. To become a consultant, the initial investment is less than $100, after which you can receive product discounts and have the opportunity to share Cell Tech products with others. All new Distributors begin at the Member title. This allows you to be eligible to receive a 5% commission on the purchases you make, and on the purchases made by any team members you enroll. As you attain higher titles, the percentage you receive on those purchases can increase to a full 25%.

Company: Cell Tech, 565 Century Court, Klamath Falls, OR 97601. Tel: 800-800-1300 or 541-883-8848. Fax: 800-797-8228. Web: www.celltech.com

Products: Super Blue Green® Algae, and skin care and nutritional supplements

Years in Business: Since 1974

Countries of Operation: U.S. and Canada

Starter Kit/Start-Up Costs: $100

Sales Method: Direct sales

Training: Upline sponsors, national training events

Online Shop Available? No

Commissions: 5–25% commission on sales

Downline Structure: 5–15% on downline sales

Incentives and Bonuses: Cash bonuses

Inventory: No

Territories: No

Quotas: Minimum purchases for discounts

Member of DSA? No

Contact a Representative!

Linda Dewing, Principal, A Vital Life, Rhode Island.
E-mail: avitallife@earthlink.net. Web: www.a-vital-life.com.

Country Bunny Bath & Body

Country Bunny specializes in bath and body products created with recipes by Founder and Owner Nancy Bogart. Country Bunny products are family-friendly with lines for women, babies, children, teens, and men. The products are free of mineral oil and petroleum. Independent Representatives ("Bunnies") can join Country Bunny Bath & Body for $179, which includes the company's corporate support service, a free Web site for one year, an online training center, and a starter kit containing catalogs and products. Bunnies can sell at Spa Shows, crafts fairs, and online. Training is provided through monthly training calls and an annual convention ("Bunnyvention"). Representatives earn 15% commission on sales, plus 5–10% on downline sales. Country Bunny has been in business since 2000.

Company: Country Bunny Bath and Body, 1106 Eaglecrest, Nixa, MO 65714. Tel: 877-665-8669 or 417-724-9690. E-mail: atyourservice@cbunny.com. Web: www.cbunny.com.

Products: Bath and body products

Years in Business: Since 2000

Countries of Operation: U.S.

Starter Kit/Start-Up Costs: $179, which includes a Web site for one year, online training center, corporate training, catalogs, business cards, order forms, and products with a tote bag.

Sales Method: Home parties (Spa Shows), online, craft fairs

Training: Online and corporate training available

Online Shop Available? Yes

Commissions: 15% commission on sales

Downline Structure: 5–10% downline commissions

Incentives and Bonuses: Trips, jewelry, sales tools

Inventory: No

Territories: No

Quotas: Must sell $300 every 6 months to remain active.

Member of DSA? Yes

Contact a Representative!

Kathleen Till, Independent Representative, Renton, WA.
E-mail: ktill@bunnymart.com. Web: www.cbunnyrep.com/4924.

Demarle at Home

DeMarle at Home specializes in kitchen gadgets, tools, and accessories aimed at making creative cooking simple, and specializes in the "Flexipan," a unique non-stick baking pan. DeMarle Representatives demonstrate these products at home parties are called "Rendex-Vous." DeMarle at Home has approximately 5,150 representatives worldwide. The starter kit is $149.95 with an opportunity to receive $149.95 reimbursement within the first 40 days of initial start date. The starter kit includes 10 products, including a flower mold flexipan, large muffin tray, stainless mixing bowl, ergonomic whisk, heat resistant spatula, beechwood rolling pin, and recipe binder with cards. Also included are marketing materials, including catalogs, brochures, and a training video. Commissions are 20–31%, with 2–11% commission override on recruits.

Company: DeMarle at Home, 5601 Slauson Avenue, Culver City, CA 90230. Tel: 310-568-1731. Fax: 310-568-8747. E-mail: info@demarleathome.com. Web: www.demarleathome.com.

Products: Specializes in a unique silicone product called the "Flexipan," as well as stainless cookware and professional knives.

Years in Business: Since 2003

Countries of Operation: U.S., France, Germany, UK, Netherlands, Belgium

Starter Kit/Start-Up Costs: $149.95 with an opportunity to receive $149.95 reimbursement within the first 40 days of initial start date. Starter kit includes 10 products, including a flower mold flexipan, large muffin tray, medium silpat, stainless mixing bowl, ergonomic whisk, heat resistant spatula, beechwood rolling pin, and recipe binder with cards. Also included are marketing materials, including catalogs, brochures, and training video.

Sales Method: Home parties

Training: Bridge calls available once a week. Company sponsored on-site training. Smart Start Guide. Conventions twice a year.

Online Shop Available? Not at this time

Commissions: 20–31% commission on sales

Downline Structure: Commission overrides are 2–11%.

Incentives and Bonuses: Free product in first 100 days of sales; incentive trips, and business building tools

Inventory: No

Territories: No

Quotas: Must remain active to be paid commissions on downline at representative and leadership levels.

Member of DSA? Yes

Contact a Representative!

Jessica Masserant, Founding Director, Bronze Chef Representative, Fowlerville, MI. Tel: (586) 419-5547. Fax: (517) 947-6188. E-mail: JessicaMasserant@juno.com. Web: www.demarleathome.com.

Discovery Toys, Inc.

Discovery Toys is about "kid powered play." They specialize in toys and games that are educational, developmental, and fun. The company has been in business for more than 25 years, and has expanded into a line of books and software. DT's Educational Consultants earn 25–50% commission on sales and 7–15% on team members. The Intro Kit costs $149 (although they offer discounted kits often) and includes fourteen of their best-selling products, as well as 25 catalogs and all of the supplies and training materials you'll need to get started. Discovery Toys have won many awards, including Parenting Awards, Dr. Toy Awards, Parent's Guide Awards, and Parent's Choice Awards.

Company: Discovery Toys, 6400 Brisa Street, Livermore, CA 94550. Tel: 800-426-4777 or 925-606-2600. Fax" 925-447-0226. E-mail: contactdt@discoverytoys.net. Web: www.discoverytoysinc.com.

Products: Educational toys, games, and software for children

Years in Business: 24 years

Countries of Operation: US and Canada

Starter Kit/Start-Up Costs: $149, which includes an assortment of their 15 top-selling toys, catalogs, supplies, and training materials

Annual Fee to Remain a Consultant: None

Sales Method: Home parties, fairs, conferences

Training: Daily calls, annual convention

Online Shop Available? Yes

Commissions: 25–50% commission on sales

Downline Structure: 7–15% on team members

Incentives and Bonuses: Monthly prizes for sales and recruiting, trips.

Inventory: No

Territories: No

Quotas: Must sell $100 retail in 3 month period to remain active.

Company Accolades: Parenting Awards, Dr. Toy Awards, Parent's Guide Awards, and Parent's Choice Awards

Member of DSA? Yes

Contact a Representative in Your Area!

ALABAMA

Terri Lambing, Group Manager, Madison, AL. Tel: (256) 895-6722. Fax: (256) 895-6722. E-mail: ToysbyTerri@aol.com. Web: www.discoverytoyslink.com/TerriLambing.

FLORIDA

Terri Lambing, Group Manager, Madison, AL. Tel: (256) 895-6722. Fax: (256) 895-6722. E-mail: ToysbyTerri@aol.com. Web: www.discoverytoyslink.com/TerriLambing.

GEORGIA

Leslie Sams, Group Manager, Norcross, GA. Tel: (770) 446-0786. Fax: (770) 446-0786. E-mail: dtshop@bellsouth.net. Web: www.lesliestoys.com.

ILLINOIS

Julie Jones-Kloeckner, Senior Manager, O'Fallon, IL. Tel: (618) 628-2716. E-mail: jjktoys@discoverytoyslink.com. Web: www.discoverytoyslink.com/jjktoys.

KENTUCKY

Terri Lambing, Group Manager, Madison, AL. Tel: (256) 895-6722. Fax: (256) 895-6722. E-mail: ToysbyTerri@aol.com. Web: www.discoverytoyslink.com/TerriLambing.

MISSISSIPPI

Terri Lambing, Group Manager, Madison, AL. Tel: (256) 895-6722. Fax: (256) 895-6722. E-mail: ToysbyTerri@aol.com. Web: www.discoverytoyslink.com/TerriLambing.

OHIO

Karrin M. Berkowitz, Group Manager, Hudson, OH. Tel: (330) 463-5683. Fax: (330) 655-1671. E-mail: Karrin6@aol.com. Web: www.discoverytoyslink.com/karrin.

TENNESSEE

Amy Beckman, Group Manager, Memphis, TN. Tel: (901) 270-8439. E-mail: amyrenee@midsouth.rr.com. Web: www.discoverytoyslink.com/amystoys.

Enchanting Scents Designs

Enchanting Scents Designs (ESD) is a direct selling company specializing in custom designed candles. Their candles are made from 100% natural soy wax. Each Candle is triple scented which allows the scent to last hours after the candle is extinguished. Enchanting Scents Designs, located in rural Madison, Ohio, was founded in the spring of 1998. Their president, Lisa Anaya, frustrated with paying high prices for low quality candles, began experimenting in her family's kitchen. After a few failed attempts, extensive research and lots of practice, she developed the recipes they use today. In a few short years, the company have grown to distribute their products across the United States and Canada through its 100 distributors. Distributors earn 30–33% commission on sales. The starter kit is free and includes training manuals and business documents.

Company: Enchanting Scents Designs, 1510 Easton Avenue, Madison, OH 44057. Tel: 440-428-3961. Fax: 530-463-8637. E-mail: escents@ncweb.com. Web: www.esdsoycandles.com.

Products: Candles made from 100% natural soy wax

Years in Business: Since 1998

Countries of Operation: U.S. and Canada

Starter Kit/Start-Up Costs: Free

Annual Fee to Remain a Consultant: None

Sales Method: Home parties

Training: Upline training, manual

Online Shop Available? No

Commissions: 30–33% commission on sales

Downline Structure: 3% on downline sales

Incentives and Bonuses: Quarterly bonuses

Inventory: No

Territories: No

Quotas: None

Member of DSA? No

Contact a Representative in Your Area!

IDAHO

Jamie Ballard, Meridian, ID. Tel: (208) 866-5001. Fax: (208) 855-2298. E-mail: sjballard@ballardandco.com. Web: www.enchantingscents4u.com.

INDIANA

Kathy Everman, Indiana. E-mail: kathye@kss4help.com.
Web: kathysshopsandservices.wahmbiz.com/shopwkathy.

FemOne

FemOne sells nutritionals, cosmetics, and weight loss products that balance and enhance health and beauty. The company has been in business since 2002. FemOne Consultants receive a 30% discount on products, a personalized e-commerce Web site to sell retail products, and a virtual office to order business cards and organize contacts. There are two options to become a FemOne Business Associate. The Welcome Kit is $24.95 and contains the Welcome Binder only. The FemOne Consultant Manager Kit is $1,000 and contains approximately $1,447 worth of products as well as the *FemOne Welcome Binder* that contains company and product information, order forms, and training materials.

Company: FemOne, 5600 Avenida Encinas, Suite 130, Carlsbad, CA 92008. Tel: 760-448-2498. Fax: 760-454-4511. E-mail: support@femone.com. Web: www.femone.com.

Products: Nutritionals, cosmetics, and weight loss products

Years in Business: Since 2002

Starter Kit/Start-Up Costs: $24.95–$49.95, includes training materials.

Sales Method: Parties

Training: Upline sponsor and manual

Online Shop Available? Yes

Commissions: 30% commission on sales

Downline Structure: Senior consultants receive 15% on first line recruits and 5% on second line recruits.

Inventory: No

Territories: No

Member of DSA? No

Contact a Representative!

Sheila Harrison, Independent Business Associate, Studio City, CA. Tel: (877) 336-6634. E-mail: sheila@myfemone.com. Web: www.myfemone.com/sheila.

For Your Pleasure, Inc.

For Your Pleasure began as Rainbow Resource, a New Hampshire-based company providing online and mail order products to the adult community. Due to increasing requests for an intimate setting for demonstrating products, lotions, and novelties, the wholesale home party division was born. For Your Pleasure began calling the home parties For Your Pleasure Parties. In 1999 For Your Pleasure developed it's streamlined Party Plan and did away with lugging the store. This provided a work smarter…not harder atmosphere for the Independent Business Associates affiliated with FYP.

For Your Pleasure is growing by leaps and bounds which is reflective of the current demand for Adult Home Parties to be provided in a private setting. With many years in business, For Your Pleasure is providing a structure for entrepreneurs to build businesses of their own. Their corporate offices and warehouse cover 15,000 sq ft on 2 levels.

The President and CEO of For Your Pleasure has more than 25 years in business, sales, marketing and finance. This provides the solid framework by which For Your Pleasure Inc. is run. With years of consulting in business, their CEO has demonstrated ability in many areas, including the ability to perform home parties and build large organizations with success.

FYP features a tasteful collection of products to enhance the romantic palette. With more than 1,200 products and a 104-page color catalog there is a selection sure to peak the interest of any intimate partner.

Company: For Your Pleasure, Inc., P.O. Box 3452, Concord, NH 03302. Tel: 603-225-8826. Fax: 603-225-3199. Email: info@foryourpleasure.com. Web: www.foryourpleasure.com

Products: Romance enhancement and adult novelties

Years in Business: Since 1999

Countries of Operation: U.S.

Starter Kit/Start-Up Costs: There are two ways to start up with For Your Pleasure. Purchasing a kit at $250, $500, or $1000 (receiving double the amount paid) or earning the kit for free through an Open For Business Show.

Annual Fee to Remain a Consultant: None

Sales Method: Direct Sales, Home Shows, and through the Web (sites can be purchased through the company, or you can create your own and link to the Online store).

Training: Independent Business Association (IBA) Manual, sponsors, online message board, and home office

Online Shop Available? Yes

Commissions: Up to 50% commission from home shows, direct sales, and website. Earn up to another 10% for Bonus in a month.

Downline Structure: Based on Sales, not recruits. Earn up to 10% on first line, plus overrides on second, third, fourth, and fifth. Also earn an added Bonus of up to $1500 on your downline sales

Incentives and Bonuses: Recruiting, sales, and contests

Inventory: No

Territories: No

Quotas: Must sell $150 every 6 months to remain active

Member of DSA? No

Contact a Representative!

Alissa Boles, Regional Director/Independent Consultant, Anderson, IN. Tel: (765) 640-5003. E-mail: alissa@funpleasures.com. Web: www.funpleasures.com.

The Fuller Brush Company

Fuller Brush is a home care expert company. Through the years, The Fuller Brush Company has grown from one man's fiber suitcase, filled with unique custom-made brushes, to an exciting collection of home/business care and personal care products. More than 2,000 items are formed within their twelve-acre plant including: household cleaning aids, industrial cleaners, polishes and wax products, cotton and synthetic mops, floor brushes & brooms, stainless steel sponges, personal care brushes, lotions and fragrances, hair care aids, and more. The 500,000 square foot plant was completed in 1973, and today Fuller remains the major employer in the Barton County, Kansas area. Consultants earn 20–46% commission on sales. The starter kits range from free to $39.95, depending on products included.

Company: The Fuller Brush Company, One Fuller Way, Great Bend, KS 67530. Tel: 800-522-0499. Fax: 620-792-1906. E-mail: info@fuller.com. Web: www.fuller.com.

Products: Home care products

Years in Business: More than 100 years

Countries of Operation: U.S.

Starter Kit/Start-Up Costs: The starter kits range from free to $39.95, depending on products included.

Annual Fee to Remain a Consultant: $29.95

Sales Method: Online and home parties

Training: Manual

Online Shop Available? Yes

Commissions: 20–46% commission on sales

Downline Structure: 1–26% on downline sales

Inventory: No

Territories: No

Quotas: None for distributors, but $35 a month retail for Managers.

Member of DSA? Yes

Contact a Representative in Your Area!

FLORIDA

Lorian Rivers, Independent Distributor #0314640, Port Richey, FL. Toll-free: (888) 552-5054. Fax: (727) 849-2543. E-mail: Lorian@FullerBrushBiz.com. Web: www.FullerBrushBiz.com.

OREGON

Pam VanLoon, Oregon. E-mail: fullerbrushlady@momdoesitall.com. Web: http://momdoesitall.com/fuller_brush.htm.

Gabby Goodies

Mary Kuipers founded Gabby Goodies in 2001. After beginning the business as a gift basket enterprise, she discovered that most people wanted the food products available for purchase separately rather than in a basket. She came up with a gourmet foods and coffee business, one that now has almost 350 products. She decided to expand her business online and across the country using the Web site and the party plan format. Their product line includes gourmet dip mixes, beer bread mixes, gourmet coffee (whole bean and ground), cocoa mixes, creamers, brownie mixes, cookies, tea, breads, muffins, and soup.

There are now more than 650 consultants nationwide who market Gabby Goodies in various ways including, but not limited to, home parties, craft fairs, gift baskets, school bazaars, and Web sites Consultants choose which methods work best for them. Consultants receive 25% commission based on their paid sales and there are no minimums to meet. They can advance into field management levels by sponsoring other consultants and in return may qualify for free products based on monthly group sales and number of people they've sponsored. There are two starter kits that contain both product and paperwork, ranging from $29.95–$49.95. There are eight levels of upper level consultants, beginning at Consultant Coordinator and ending at Shining Star Consultant. When each level is attained, free product is awarded. The annual renewal fee if $15.

Company: Gabby Goodies, Crestwood, IL. Tel: 877-576-7666.
E-mail: gabbygoodies@aol.com. Web: www.gabbygoodies.com

Products: Gourmet foods and coffee

Years in Business: Since 2001

Countries of Operation: U.S.

Starter Kit/Start-Up Costs: $29.95–$49.95

Annual Fee to Remain a Consultant: $15

Sales Method: Home parties, craft fairs, gift baskets, school bazaars, and online

Training: Manual, sponsors

Online Shop Available? Yes

Commissions: 25%

Downline Structure: Free product awarded for achieving upper levels

Inventory: No

Territories: No

Quotas: No

Member of DSA? No

Contact a Representative!

Debbie Ciulla, Simi Valley, CA. Tel: (805) 527-6827. Fax: (805) 581-7066. E-mail: kciulla@global.net. Web: www.coffeegal.com.

Gifted Expressions

Gifted Expressions offers a selection of gourmet food gifts, spa assortments, and classic accessories. Gift Specialists do not have to purchase and stock any inventory or deliver any orders. All products are shipped from their 25,000 square-foot facility in Hartford, Connecticut within 24–48 hours. "GifTogethers" are their version of the traditional home party. Consultants earn 20% commission on sales, plus 2–7% on recruits. The starter kit is $249 (a $900 retail value) and includes gifting samples, catalogs, brochures, invitations, a training guide, and order forms. Gifted Expressions has been in business since 2003, but their parent company, Giftcorp, has been in business for 20 years.

Company: Gifted Expressions, 20–28 Sargeant Street, Hartford, CT 06105. Tel: 866-543-4438. Fax: 866-450-5566.
E-mail: customerservice@giftedexpressions.com.
Web: www.giftedexpressions.com.

Products: Gourmet food, gifts, spa assortments

Years in Business: Since 2003

Countries of Operation: U.S.

Starter Kit/Start-Up Costs: $289 (a $900 value), which includes gifting samples, catalogs, brochures, invitations, training guide, and order forms.

Annual Fee to Remain a Consultant: None

Sales Method: GifTogethers (home parties)

Training: Local sponsors, conference calls

Online Shop Available? Yes

Commissions: 20% commission on sales

Downline Structure: 2–7% on downline sales

Incentives and Bonuses: 2–5% bonuses, trips, monthly sales incentives

Inventory: No

Territories: No

Quotas: Must sell $500 every 6 months to remain active

Member of DSA? No

Contact a Representative in Your Area!

OHIO

Stephne Miller, Gift Specialist, West Chester, OH. Tel: (513) 759-5195. Fax: (513) 759-6219. E-mail: TheGiftLady@cinci.rr.com.
Web: www.GiftedExpressions.com.

VIRGINIA

Kimberly Hedrick, Gift Specialist, Fredericksburg, VA. Tel: (540) 891-4188. Fax: (540) 891-4188. E-mail: Kim4Gifting@adelphia.net.
Web: www.giftedexpressions.com.

Herbalife International, Inc.

Herbalife Distributors begin with the Herbalife International Business Pack (IBP), which costs less than $100 and includes a training manual. Herbalife's products fall into two main categories: "Inner Nutrition," which includes weight loss, essential nutrition, health supplements; energy boosters, and fitness and sports snacks/nutrition products; and "Outer Nutrition," which includes skin care and hair care products. The products are aimed at slimming down, increasing energy, de-stressing, and rejuvenating skin. Independent Distributors are trained to create customized programs for their customers, based on their Cellular Nutrition® approach. Herbalife was founded in 1980, and now has more than one million independent distributors selling Herbalife products in 58 countries worldwide.

Herbalife's distributor training and support system includes: monthly success training seminars that teach you about the business; leadership development weekends; televised product and business-building training via the Herbalife Broadcast Network; Internet support tools; annual international "Extravaganza" events for networking and training; advice from the Herbalife Medical Advisory Board and Medical Affairs Group; sales literature and promotional tools; and access to wellness training seminars. Herbalife Distributors earn 25–50% commission sales, plus 5–25% on team members.

Company: Herbalife International of America, Inc., P.O. Box 80210, Los Angeles, CA 90080-0210. Tel: 866-866-4744. Fax: 310-258-7019. Web: www.herbalife.com.

Products: Nutritionals and health products

Years in Business: Since 1980

Countries of Operation: 58 countries

Starter Kit/Start-Up Costs: $100, includes training manual

Annual Fee to Remain a Consultant: $10

Sales Method: Home parties, ads, fliers, vendor fairs, online

Training: Monthly success seminars, leadership development weekends, and wellness training seminars

Online Shop Available? Yes

Commissions: 25–50% commission on sales

Downline Structure: 5–25% on downline sales

Incentives and Bonuses: 2–6% cash bonuses

Inventory: No

Territories: No

Quotas: Small quotas apply to higher level consultants

Member of DSA? Yes

Contact a Representative!

Nancy French, Herbalife Independent Distributor, San Antonio, TX. Tel: (210) 382-7909. E-mail: nanzlifeline@satx.rr.com.

Home and Garden Party

Home and Garden Party features a range of home decorating items, including framed prints, candle assortments, lotions and shower gels, decorative accessories, figurines, garden items, bakeware products, and a line of pottery and stoneware. They have more than 26,000 Designers in the U.S.

Company: Home and Garden Party, Ltd. 2938 Brown Rd., Marshall, TX 75672. Tel: 903-935-4197. Fax: 903-935-3170. E-mail: customerservice@hgcorp.net. Web: www.homeandgardenparty.com.

Products: Home decorating items, including framed prints, candle assortments, lotions and shower gels, decorative accessories, figurines, garden items, bakeware products, and a line of pottery and stoneware.

Years in Business: 8 years

Countries of Operation: U.S.

Starter Kit/Start-Up Costs: Kit costs $150 and includes products to display with a retail value of more than $300, as well as business supplies.

Annual Fee to Remain a Consultant: $25

Sales Method: Home parties and fundraisers.

Training: Training CDs and literature with sample kit. Phone and Internet training available monthly. Regional training meetings held across the US at various sites, as well as a National Rally every year.

Online Shop Available? Yes

Commissions: 30–40% commission on sales

Downline Structure: 3–6% on recruit sales, plus a 10% sponsoring bonus on a recruits' initial $1,500 in sales.

Incentives and Bonuses: Contests throughout the year are offered with prizes that include trips, prizes, and products. They also offer a Ladder of Leadership program that features cash bonuses.

Inventory: No

Territories: No

Quotas: Not for earning personal commissions, but to receive commissions on downline sales, Designers must sell at least $300 within a given month.

Company Accolades: Home and Garden Party has contributed more then $400,000 to the American Cancer Society in the last three years. They also support the Boys and Girls Clubs, the Humane Society, the United Way, and Habitat for Humanity. They are sponsors of the nationally recognized Entrepreneurship Program at Baylor University.

Member of DSA? Previously a member, and may be rejoining.

Contact a Representative in Your Area!

ALABAMA

Karen Long, Diamond Designer, Hazel Green, AL. Tel: (256) 829-1210. Fax: (256) 829-1210. E-mail: ilovehgp@mchsi.com. Web: www.homeandgardenparty.com.

OREGON

Kent & Jackie Shappart, Independent Designers, Oregon. Tel: (541) 726-8766. E-mail: jackie@hgp4me.com. Web: www.ghp4me.com.

The Homemaker's Idea Company

For more than 32 years, The Homemaker's Idea Company has been selling a complete line of organizing and decorating essentials, including baskets, linens, florals, greens, pottery, and wallpaper borders through home parties. Products come under several categories: Casual Living; Bridal and Inspiration; Bathin' Beauty; Entertain in Style; Romantic Spaces; Store 'n' More; Comfortable Classics; Escape from the Ordinary; Kid's Style; and That Extra Touch. Consultants earn 25% commission of retail. The starter case is $175, and can be returned within one year for a 90% refund. The kit contains $500 worth of products and training materials.

Company: The Homemaker's Idea Company, 500 Wall St., Glendale Heights, IL 60139. Tel: 800-800-5452. E-mail: info@homemakersidea.com.
Web: www.homemakersideacompany.com.

Products: Organizing and decorating products

Years in Business: 32 years

Countries of Operation: U.S.

Starter Kit/Start-Up Costs: $175 (a $500 value), and includes training materials and product samples.

Annual Fee to Remain a Consultant: None

Sales Method: Home parties

Training: Monthly team meetings, training manual, videos, CDs, e-mail support, upline training

Online Shop Available? Yes

Commissions: 25% commission on sales

Downline Structure: Not available at this time

Incentives and Bonuses: Monthly cash bonuses

Inventory: No

Territories: No

Quotas: None. Reps are removed as active if no sales for 1 year.

Member of DSA? No

Contact a Representative!

Angie Cyr, Independent Sales Manager, California. Toll-free: (800) 715-9083. E-mail: info@love2organize.com. Web: www.BeThere4Them.com.

HomeWare Creations

HomeWare Creations opened its doors in March 2003, and has been under new management since February 2004. Its business opportunity is scheduled to re-launch in July 2004. They presently have 100 Associates in 30 states with three levels attainable: Associate, Lead Associate, and Director. Associates earn 20% commission on sales, while Fundraiser Specialists earn 15% commission. In addition, Associates may purchase products at 50% off. Homeware Creations has a free start-up option where you commit to four home parties and that from the third and fourth party commissions you repay $125 to offset the cost of the startup kit (which is a $300 value).

Company: HomeWare Creations, Administrative Office, 447 Fulton Street, Suite 200, Waverly, NY 14901. Tel: 607-565-8953. Fax: 607-565-8991. E-mail: contactus@homewarecreations.com. Web: www.homewarecreations.com.

Products: Bradbury Baskets©, Nestlings©, Stay Fresh© containers, Vitrix© Porcelain, and other household items.

Years in Business: Since 2003

Countries of Operation: U.S. and U.S. Territories. Possible expansion into Canada in 2005.

Starter Kit/Start-Up Costs: Starter kit is $125 (a $300 value) and includes current products, 5 catalogs, order forms, business-growth brochures, current newsletter, and the Associate Manual. A payment option is available where new consultants receive their kit for free, then submit their commissions earned over the first two months to pay for the kit.

Sales Method: Home parties, direct selling, online, fairs, consignment shops, and other methods determined by Associates

Training: Upline training, online chats, scheduled e-mail, and monthly newsletters

Online Shop Available? Yes

Commissions: 20% commission on sales, 15% commission from fundraisers. 50% discount on personal orders

Downline Structure: 3% commission on first line recruits

Incentives and Bonuses: Sales and coaching bonuses

Inventory: No

Territories: No

Quotas: Quotas required of Lead Associates and Directors.

Member of DSA? No

Contact a Representative!

Kelly Flynn, Fundraiser Director & Associate/Director, Elmira, NY. Tel: (607) 737-7538. Fax: (607) 737-7538. E-mail: KFlynn@HWCNewYork.com. Web: www.HWCNewYork.com.

Joielle Fine Jewelry

Joielle® (JOY-EL) is a manufacturer and distributor of fine jewelry. The name Joielle means "bringing joy to her." The company was founded by Michael Posternak and his two brothers, Martin and Daniel, who wanted to start a new business that would create high quality, fashionable, affordable fine jewelry to be distributed exclusively through independent Jewelry Consultants at home demonstrations. Their dream became the company, Joielle. The Joielle collection consists of 400 fine jewelry pieces handcrafted by worldwide designers in sterling silver and accented with 14k gold, gemstones, and genuine pearls. The Joielle designer signature is featured on the jewelry collections. Joielle also stands behind each product with a Lifetime Quality Guarantee. Consultants earn 25% to 40% commission on jewelry sales, plus 2.5% to 20% on team members.

The business kit costs $120, and includes one of their most popular bangle bracelets, a pair of earrings, a piece of peridot, Joielle first year registration; a Joielle home page; Joielle catalogs; invitation postcards; Joielle gift box and roll; anti-tarnish velvet pouches; opportunity brochures; hostess and guest order forms; registration agreements; the consultant "Guide to Success" manual; a ring sizer; plus a one-time discount on demonstration jewelry, up to 65% off retail.

Company: Joielle Fine Jewelry. Tel: 866-994-7370. Web: www.joielle.com.

Products: Jewelry

Starter Kit/Start-Up Costs: $120, which includes 3 pieces of demo jewelry, home page, catalogs, invitations, anti-tarnish velvet pouches, brochures, order forms, registration agreements, training manual, ring sizer, plus a one-time discount on additional demonstration jewelry (65% off retail).

Sales Method: Home parties

Training: Upline sponsor and consultant manual

Online Shop Available? Yes

Commissions: 25–40% commission on sales

Downline Structure: 2½-20% commission on team members

Inventory: No

Territories: No

Member of DSA? Yes

Contact a Representative in Your Area!

HAWAII

Christiane Bolosan-Yee, Founding Independent Jewelry Consultant, Ewa Beach, HI. Tel: (808) 778-3230. E-mail: christianesjewels@hotmail.com. Web: www.joielle.com/online/christiane.htm.

WASHINGTON

Kathy Leistikow, Independent Sales Consultant, Lynnwood, WA. Tel: (425) 238-1454. E-mail: cathyscharms@aol.com. Web: www.cathyscharms.com.

MINNESOTA

Lauren Eberhart, Founding Independent Jewelry Consultant, Minnestrista, MN. Tel: (612) 867-2267. Fax: (952) 495-8142. E-mail: leberhart@frontiernet.net.

Mary Kay Cosmetics

Mary Kay Inc. is one of the largest direct sellers of skin care and color cosmetics in the world. Mary Kay Independent Beauty Consultants number more than 1.1 million and represent more than 30 markets worldwide. Mary Kay Inc. was founded in 1963. The Mary Kay® product line includes more than 200 products in seven categories: facial skin care, color cosmetics, nail care, body care, sun protection, fragrances, and men's skin care.

For more than 40 years, the company has applied Mary Kay's philosophy of God first, family second and career third. Mary Kay Inc. was created to provide an open-ended opportunity for women. The company encourages building a successful business while living a balanced life—a philosophy that continues to thrive after 40 years. The Mary Kay Inc. World Headquarters is located in North Dallas and totals nearly 600,000 square feet and employs approximately 3,600 Mary Kay Inc. employees.

In the United States, starting a Mary Kay business costs less than $100 for a complete product demonstration kit and educational materials. Online shopping and ordering can be customized for Independent Beauty Consultants on their individual Mary Kay Web sites.

Incentives includes the legendary Mary Kay Career Car Program (the legendary pink Cadillac), as well as computer equipment and luxurious trips. The Mary Kay Career Car Program includes nearly 10,000 U.S. cars. In addition to the Cadillac, the program includes the Pontiac Grand Prix and the Pontiac Grand Am. Since the inception of the Career Car Program, Mary Kay Inc. has awarded the use of more than 80,000 cars to its independent sales force. International car programs feature Mercedes, BMWs, Toyotas and Fords.

Facials and skin care classes are the basics of a Mary Kay business. Classes are called "On the Face" appointments, as well as "On the Go" appointments, which are quick, 15-minute sessions for customer with little time to spare. Beauty Consultants earn 50% commission on sales, plus 4–26% on downline sales.

Company: Mary Kay Cosmetics, P.O. Box 799045, Dallas, TX 75379-9045. Tel: 800-627-9529. Web: www.marykay.com.

Products: Skin care and cosmetics

Years in Business: Since 1963

Countries of Operation: U.S. and Internationally

Starter Kit/Start-Up Costs: $100

Annual Fee to Remain a Consultant: None

Sales Method: Facials and skin care classes

Training: Weekly local meetings, annual regional and national meetings, CDs/cassettes, videos, online, and special events

Online Shop Available? Yes

Commissions: 50% commission on sales

Downline Structure: 4–26% on downline sales

Incentives and Bonuses: Career car program, computer equipment, trips.

Inventory: No

Territories: No

Quotas: Must sell $200 wholesale per quarter to remain active.

Member of DSA? Yes

Contact a Representative in Your Area!

CALIFORNIA

Debbie Novak, Independent Beauty Consultant, West Hills, CA. Tel: (818) 974-8951. E-mail: debbiecnovak@marykay.com. Web: www.marykay.com/debbienovak.

DELAWARE

Debbie Baker, Independent Beauty Consultant, Millsboro, DE. Tel: (302) 945-3687. E-mail: skincareteacher@yahoo.com. Web: www.marykay.com/debbiebaker.

INDIANA

Jill Velikan, Independent Beauty Consultant, Avon, IN. Tel: (317) 272-5719. E-mail: jvelikan1@yahoo.com. Web: www.marykay.com/jvelikan.

SOUTH CAROLINA

Mary Grove, Sales Director, Port Royal, SC. Tel: (843) 252-3478. Fax: (843) 986-1082. E-mail: mgrove1@marykay.com. Web: www.marykay.com/mgrove1.

TEXAS

Julieanna Walker. E-mail: julieannawalker@sbcglobal.net. Web: www.marykay.com/julieannawalker.

VIRGINIA

Mary Beth Henry, Senior Sales Director, Herndon, VA. Tel: (703) 766-0294. E-mail: mhenry2@marykay.com. Web: www.marykay.com/mhenry2.

My Precious Kid

My Precious Kid specializes in ID cards for children that provide basic medical information, fingerprints, emergency contact names, and a medical release signature. The company was formed because of the need for children's safety products that can save a child's life. In addition to the value of recording your child's DNA and fingerprint information (just in case), an official looking ID card is readily accepted by libraries, community centers, the airport and other organizations. Plus, identification helps in the return of lost car seats, strollers, wheelchairs, wagons, diapers bags, and back packs. We all hope to never have missing children. Children's safety ID cards and fingerprint kits are like insurance just in case.

To become a rep, the $30 initial package contains one $16 sample Child Safety Pack, as well as a flyer, order form, catalog, name tag, product display board, sales manual, calendar, promo order form, mileage log, and stickers and sample letter (contents vary from time to time). The $30 also covers the cost of setting up your rep account and wholesale buying status. The optional additional New Rep Sample Pack is $94 and contains one of each of their 17 products (ID/DNA/FP Kit, Child Safety Pack, DNA/FP Kit, Wallet Kit, Luggage Tag Kit, Car Seat Kit, Pet Kit, Bracelets, Medical Kit, Adult Kit, Shoe Stickers, Spanish Kit, Chore Chart, Medicine Chart, Shoe Tags, Boo Boo Box, and Kid Scope) and is a $188.00 value.

Reps can buy any of their ID card products wholesale and resell to customers receiving 50% off retail when they buy the $50 minimum ($100 retail). Consultants receive 25% profit on smaller orders and drop-shipped orders. Profit on non-ID-kit items (not made by MPK) is 25–30%. Plus, there is 5% commission on downline sales. You must have ordered $50 wholesale each month to receive your downline commission.

My Precious Kid has 100 sales reps in the U.S. and Canada, and created their first ID card product in May 2001.

Company: My Precious Kid™, P.O. Box 271, Banks, OR 97106-0271.Tel: 503-324-7323. Fax: 775-667-6323. E-mail: Kay@mypreciouskid.com. Web: www.MyPreciousKid.com.

Products: 25+ safety items including: ID cards, DNA, fingerprint kits, pet Ids, shoe ID sticker and tags, ID bracelets, baby slings, luggage tags, medical release cards, car seat ID cards, travel totes, sports packs, safety books, and medical record books, priced at $5–$30 each.

Years in Business: 3 years

Countries of Operation: U.S. and Canada

Starter Kit/Start-Up Costs: Initial kit costs $30. Optional $94 sample kit is also available.

Annual Fee to Remain a Consultant: None

Sales Method: Direct selling

Training: Consultant manual

Online Shop Available? No

Commissions: 25–50% commission on sales

Downline Structure: 5% commission on direct recruits

Incentives and Bonuses: Occasional incentives vary

Inventory: Optional.

Territories: No

Quotas: Must order one item every 90 days

Company Accolades: My Precious Kid was recently featured in *Woman's Day* magazine and *Home Business* magazine.

Member of DSA? No

Contact a Representative in Your Area!

OREGON

Pam VanLoon, Executive Rep Manager, E-mail: mpkpam@momdoesitall.com. Web: http://momdoesitall.com/mpk.htm.

PENNSYLVANIA

Kathy Hoover-Rutt, Owner, Colorful Collections.org, Rep. #KR362, Camp Hill, PA. Tel: (717) 732-9188. E-mail: Kathy@ColorfulCollections.org. Web: www.ColorfulCollections.org.

Northern Lights at Home

Northern Lights at Home was founded in 1978 by Andres and Christina Glanzman when they produced original wax designs in their small Western New York workshop and marketed them at local art and craft shows. Today, NLAH sells candles through independent presenters and the At Home Division is represented in more than 41 states. In 2003 the company celebrated its 25th anniversary. They offer their Presenters ongoing training and business building ideas and aids. All their products have a 30 day money-back guarantee. Presenters earn 30% commission on sales, plus a 5% monthly bonus. Incentives include gifts and vacations.

A short timeline:

1978: Northern Lights Candles founded by Andrew and Christina Glanzman.

1989: Placed on the prestigious Inc. 500 list as one of the fastest growing companies in the United States. Number one selling candles in Japan.

1995: Company stores expanded to 40 locations across the US and Canada. Additional 15,000 square foot warehouse and another office extension added.

1996: Built 10,000 square foot wax melting facility. President Andy Glanzman listed in directory of Who's Who of American Entrepreneurs. Staff increased to over 400 employees during the peak of the holiday season.

1998: New division, Northern Lights at Home was started. Northern Lights Candles celebrates their twenty-year-anniversary.

1999: At Home Division signs its one hundredth Presenter in November. Construction began on 12,750 square foot production facility expansion project.

2001: At Home Division becomes an official member of the Direct Selling Association (DSA) in December. Installed new automated manufacturing equipment to increase capacity and efficiency.

2003: Northern Lights Candles celebrates their twenty-five-year anniversary. At Home Division is represented in over 41 states.

Company: Northern Lights at Home, 3474 Andover Road, Wellsville, NY 14895. Tel: 585-593-1200. Fax: 585-593-6481. E-mail: info@northernlightsathome.com. Web: www.northernlightsathome.com.

Products: Candles

Years in Business: Since 1978

Countries of Operation: U.S.

Starter Kit/Start-Up Costs: Three starter kits are $149, $199, and $249. Each includes an assortment of candles and accessories, catalogs, brochures, invitations, delivery bags, manual, order forms, a personal planner, questionnaires, and a training video.

Annual Fee to Remain a Consultant: None

Sales Method: Home parties, direct selling

Training: Consultant manual, training video, upline sponsor

Online Shop Available? No

Commissions: 30–35% commission on sales

Inventory: No

Territories: No

Quotas: No

Member of DSA? Yes

Contact a Representative!

Michele Mitchell, Londonderry, NH. Tel: (603) 432-5943. E-mail: michelemitchell@adelphia.net.

Nouveau Cosmeceuticals

Nouveau Cosmeceuticals is dedicated to skin wellness, not just skin care. Nouveau has combined the best of your typical cosmetics with the best of the pharmaceutical industry's skin rejuvenation materials and has created a regimen that promotes the health of your skin.

As Cosmeceuticals, and not merely cosmetics, Nouveau products interact with your skin to penetrate and affect the structure of damaged skin. Typical anti-aging systems work by exfoliating the skin but do nothing to stimulate or promote cell growth. Nouveau goes beyond the typical anti-aging system by making products that work in tandem to create a new skin wellness system.

The Complete Nouveau System was formulated to work for people from 8 to 80 years old, for all skin types, and all races. The objective behind their formulations is to 1) cleanse the skin and kill bacteria, 2) stimulate the skin by adding acid or organic alcohol, and 3) protect and moisturize. Nouveau's products have been designed to work in harmony with each other and represent a marriage of three different classes of materials: a wrinkle eliminator, a collagen stimulator and a cell rejuvenator.

The Complete Nouveau System is a super-exfoliating system and, at the same time, a sub-cellular skin building system. The product works both by exfoliating the outer surface of the skin, removing dead skin cells while, at the same time, stimulating the body's natural systems to produce new proteins that support the sub-cellular cells. Simply put, Nouveau works by making the skin act and function as if it were years younger.

Company: Nouveau Cosmeceuticals, LLC, 1746 West Crosby Road, Carrollton, TX 75006. Tel: 877-296-6883. Web: www.bynouveau.com.

Products: Skin wellness products

Years in Business: Since 2002

Countries of Operation: U.S. and U.S. Territories

Starter Kit/Start-Up Costs: The Executive Starter Kit is $249 (a retail value of more than $450) and includes a Consultant ID number, online manual, 2 complete Nouveau Systems, 2 Nouveau Slimming and Regenerating Body Systems, 25 Nouveau Cosmeceutical Brochures, 25 Nouveau Body Cosmeceutical Brochures, the option to enroll in the monthly Executive Autoship Program. As an Executive Consultant, you have the option to subscribe to a personal

WebStore, complete with Virtual Office, at a discounted rate. The Basic Starter Kit is $49.95 and includes consultant ID number, online manual, and the option to enroll in the monthly Executive Autoship Program.

Annual Fee to Remain a Consultant: None

Sales Method: Direct selling, Internet sales and home parties

Training: Online training manual and upline training, as well as a dedicated Corporate support team

Online Shop Available? Yes

Commissions: 45% commission on retail sales

Downline Structure: 2–8% commission on downline sales

Incentives and Bonuses: Quarterly Executive Leadership Bonus Pool

Inventory: No

Territories: No

Quotas: No

Company Accolades: With first year sales in excess of $750,000, the company closed out its largest sales month ever in April 2004 and has been experiencing steady growth since its opening in November 2002.

Member of DSA? Pending Member

Contact a Representative!

Sandy Stewart, Executive Manager #1009, Reading, PA. Toll-free: 800-670-7278. E-mail: SpecialSkin@comcast.net. Web: www.SpecialSkin.com.

Nu Skin International

Nu Skin specializes in personal care products with an emphasis on skin care. Founded in 1984, Nu Skin has expanded into more than 30 markets worldwide with over 550,000 active distributors. They produce products in skin care, ethnobotanicals, hair care, cosmetics, fragrance, and oral care products. The company started in 1984 with a commitment to provide skin care formulations that feature premium, wholesome ingredients with no unfriendly fillers. The company has partnerships with the Stanford University School of Medicine and the Nu Skin Professional Advisory Board. Nu Skin distributes through person-to-person marketing. The starter kits range from $99–$398, depending on the products included. Consultants earn 25–33% commission on sales, plus 6–12% in downline sales. Training is provided about the products through sponsors and conference calls. Bonus points can be earned for free products.

Company: Nu Skin International, Inc., One NuSkin Plaza, 75 West Center Street, Provo, UT 84601. Tel: 801-345-1000. Fax: 801-345-2799. E-mail: contactus@nuskin.com. Web: www.nuskin.com.

Products: Personal and skin care products

Years in Business: Since 1984

Countries of Operation: 30 countries

Starter Kit/Start-Up Costs: $99–$398, depending on products included.

Annual Fee to Remain a Consultant: None

Sales Method: Home parties, online

Training: Product training and conference calls

Online Shop Available? Yes

Commissions: 25–33% commission on sales

Downline Structure: 6–12% on downline sales

Incentives and Bonuses: Bonus points for free products and bonus pool

Inventory: No

Territories: No

Quotas: Quotas only for higher levels of consultant

Member of DSA? Yes

Contact a Representative!

Pattie Stalons, Frostproof, FL. Tel: (863) 635-3485. E-mail: pattie@bigplanet.com. Web: www.getresults.mynuskin.com.

Once Upon a Charm...®

Founded in Provo, Utah, Once Upon A Charm...® is a nationwide direct sales company selling sterling silver charms and bracelets. Each charm can represent a special memory or event from your life. They offer more than 1,200 sterling silver charms to choose from, a variety of sterling silver bracelets, necklaces, and their one of a kind Once Upon A Charm...® Storybook™. Once Upon A Charm...® is a unique way for you to capture the little things in life that have brought you joy and be able to share those memories with others.

The starter kit is $130 and includes 20 product samples of their most popular charms, 2 sample bracelets, 12 catalogs, a display system, and business supplies. Commission is 22% on sales, plus 2–3% on downline sales. Training is available through the manual, consultant news, consultant meetings, and upline training. Products and business tools are awarded monthly for sales volumes.

Company: Once Upon A Charm, P.O. Box 971152, Orem, UT 84097. Tel: 866-6CHARMS or 801-370-3482. Fax: 801-607-3416.
E-mail: onceuponacharm@comcast.net. Web: www.onceuponacharm.com.

Products: Charm jewelry

Years in Business: Since 2001

Countries of Operation: U.S.

Starter Kit/Start-Up Costs: $130, which includes 20 charm samples, 2 sample bracelets, 12 catalogs, a display system, and all paperwork.

Annual Fee to Remain a Consultant: None

Sales Method: Home shows

Training: Consultant manual, monthly consultant news, consultant meetings, and upline training

Online Shop Available? No

Commissions: 22% commission on sales

Downline Structure: 2–3% on downline sales

Incentives and Bonuses: No

Inventory: No

Territories: No

Quotas: Must sell $250 retail per quarter to remain active

Member of DSA? No

Contact a Representative!

Annette Yen, Illinois. E-mail: annetteyen@aol.com.

Once Upon a Family

Once Upon a Family specializes in a variety of specialty scrapbooks, albums, and family tree accessories designed to make preserving memories easy and important. The products fall under several categories:

- **Childhood Cherished** (A coordinated grouping of keepsakes and baby books that trace each milestone in a child's life)
- **Staying in Touch** (heirloom quality family tree books, note cards, and journals)
- **Celebrating Family** (beautiful photo album collection, family calendar, and memory board)
- **Treasured Traditions** (holiday traditions and photo books, one book for every month of the year, as well as Holiday Tradition Sacks that can help you get started on some new traditions)
- **Family Celebrations** (special occasions albums)
- **Gifts of Love** (love notes and love tags).

Once Upon A Family Consultants earn up to 25% profit on every sale. Their Celebrations (home parties) are designed to help people strengthen family ties and earn income at the same time. Downline bonuses can range from an additional 2% to 8% based on the size of your organization and your earned title. Consultants also have the opportunity to achieve "Honorary Founder" status based on their sales. The starter kits are $125, $250 or $370 and include a selection of products and training materials.

Company: Once Upon a Family, 17252 Armstrong Ave, Suite B, Irvine, CA 92614. Tel: 949-250-1155. Fax: 949-955-0665. Web: www.onceuponafamily.com.

Products: Scrapbooks, photo albums, family tree books, and more

Years in Business: Since 2002

Countries of Operation: U.S.

Starter Kit/Start-Up Costs: Starter kits are $125, $250 or $370.

Annual Fee to Remain a Consultant: None

Sales Method: Home parties

Training: Upline sponsors, corporate training, teleconference calls, weekend events

Online Shop Available? Yes

Commissions: Up to 25% commission on sales

Downline Structure: 2–8% on team members

Incentives and Bonuses: Monthly incentives, commission increases, free products, spa weekends, cruises

Inventory: No

Territories: No

Quotas: No (if no activity for one year, removed as active consultant)

Member of DSA? No

Contact a Representative in Your Area!

ARIZONA

Michele Ogden, Founding Director. E-mail: micheleogden@hotmail.com. Web: www.onceuponafamily.com/michele.

ARKANSAS

Catherine Hughes, Founding Director, Tulsa, OK. Tel: 918-745-9138. E-mail: catherine@onceuponafamily.com. Web: www.onceuponafamily.com/catherine

CALIFORNIA

Annabelle Cronk, Founding Director, Irvine, CA. Tel: (714) 665-4201. Fax: (714) 665-4201. E-mail: annabelle@onceuponafamily.com.
Web: www.onceuponafamily.com/annabelle.

GEORGIA

Lorri Williams, Honorary Founder. Toll-free: (800) 556-0702.
E-mail: lorriwilliams@comcast.net. Web: www.onceuponafamily.com/lorriwilliams.

IDAHO

Heidi Christianson, Independent Consultant, Boise, ID. Tel: (208) 353-5525.
E-mail: heidic@onceuponafamily.com. Web: www.OnceUponAFamily.com.

ILLINOIS

Mary Lou Doudican, Founding Director, Tulsa, OK. Tel: (918) 747-8999. E-mail: ouaftulsa@aol.com. Web: www.onceuponafamily.com/ouaftulsa.

INDIANA

Karla Elliott, Founding Director. E-mail: karla@onceuponafamily.com. Web: www.onceuponafamily.com/karla.

LOUISIANA

Lorri Williams, Honorary Founder. Toll-free: (800) 556-0702.
E-mail: lorriwilliams@comcast.net.
Web: www.onceuponafamily.com/lorriwilliams.

MASSACHUSETTS

Kerry Mahar. E-mail: kerrymahar@onceuponafamily.com.
Web: www.onceuponafamily.com/kerrymahar.

MICHIGAN

Mary Lou Doudican, Founding Director, Tulsa, OK. Tel: (918) 747-8999. E-mail: ouaftulsa@aol.com. Web: www.onceuponafamily.com/ouaftulsa.

MINNESOTA

Sharon Warmka. Tel: (952) 892-5702. E-mail: swarmka@aol.com. Web: www.onceuponafamily.com.net.

MISSISSIPPI

Lorri Williams, Honorary Founder, Jackson, MS. Toll-free: (800) 556-0702. E-mail: lorriwilliams@comcast.net. Web: www.onceuponafamily.com/lorriwilliams.

MISSOURI

Gina Rodriguez, Consultant, Neosho, MO. Tel: (417) 451-6707. E-mail: gina@joplin.com.

NEW YORK

Catherine Hughes, Founding Director, Tulsa, OK. Tel: 918-745-9138. E-mail: catherine@onceuponafamily.com. Web: www.onceuponafamily.com/catherine

NORTH CAROLINA

Lorri Williams, Honorary Founder. Tel: (800) 556-0702.
E-mail: lorriwilliams@comcast.net.
Web: www.onceuponafamily.com/lorriwilliams.

OKLAHOMA

Tamera Daniel, Founding Direct, Tulsa, OK. Tel: (918) 712-2854.
E-mail: tammydaniel@cox.net. Web: www.onceuponafamily.com/tamera.

TEXAS

Susan Kutac, Honorary Founding Director, Harlingen, TX. Tel: (956) 423-1749.
Fax: (956) 423-1794. E-mail: slkutac@swbell.net.
Web: www.onceuponafamily.com/skutac.

PartyLite Gifts

The quality of PartyLite candles continues a tradition set by a New England schoolteacher and entrepreneur, Mabel Baker. In 1905, Mabel began to make candles from the bayberries on Cape Cod. Her business grew and flourished for years as Colonial Candle of Cape Cod. For more about Mabel, click here.

In 1973, Colonial Candle of Cape Cod set up PartyLite Gifts, Inc. to sell excess inventory of candles from their factory and gift shop in Hyannis, Massachusetts. Today, PartyLite Gifts sells candles and candle accessories through home demonstrations and has expanded into many international markets. Consultants earn between 25–32% commission on sales, plus a 7% commission on team members. Candles are sold only through home demonstrations. The starter kit is free, and includes candles and accessories, literature, manual, show video, and catalogs. Incentives change from month to month, and include cash, product, and business tools. Established as PartyLite in 1973.

Company: PartyLite Gifts, Inc., 59 Armstrong Road, Plymouth, MA. Tel: 508-830-3100. Fax: 508-732-5818. Web: www.partylite.com.

Products: Candles and accessories

Years in Business: Since 1973

Countries of Operation: U.S.

Starter Kit/Start-Up Costs: Costs nothing to start. Kit includes candles and accessories, literature, manual, show video, and catalogs.

Sales Method: Home Demonstrations

Training: Unit meetings, regional meetings once a month, and unit workshops

Online Shop Available? No

Commissions: 25–32% commission on sales

Downline Structure: 7% commission on team members

Incentives and Bonuses: Sales and sponsoring contests

Inventory: No

Territories: No

Quotas: Must sell $500 in one month to remain active

Member of DSA? Yes

Contact a Representative!

Rachel Kerr Schneider, Regional Leader, Flower Mound, TX. Tel: (972) 539-9767. Fax: (972) 874-2949. E-mail: candlecrusader@aol.com.

Passion Parties

Passion Parties, formerly Coming Attractions Parties, Inc., was founded in 1994 to sell fun, tasteful, adult toys, sexual aids, and lingerie. They consider their approach educational, and their consultants are trained in enhancing a couple's sex life through the introduction and use of sensual products. Their Director of Professional Education and Communication, Dr. Louanne Cole-Weston, is an expert in human sexuality and helps their consultants increase their understanding of sexuality and its role in healthy relationships. The Passion Party, in the privacy of the customer's home along with her close friends, is their method of selling their sensual products in a positive, supportive environment. The parties include thoughtful descriptions of the variety of products and suggestions for use. Incentives for consultants include trips, a car program, and a yearly convention. Consultants earn 40% commission on sales, plus 3–5% on downline sales, and can also earn monthly cash bonuses. Starter kits are available for $100, $250, or $450, and include products, catalogs, order forms, a training video, and a business manual.

Company: Passion Parties, 440 Valley Drive, Brisbane, CA 94005. Tel: 800-4PASSION or 415-656-2161. Fax: 415-656-2164. Web: www.passionparties.com.

Products: Adult toys, sexual aids, and lingerie

Years in Business: Since 1994

Countries of Operation: U.S. and Canada

Starter Kit/Start-Up Costs: $250–$450, includes products, catalogs, order forms, training video, and business manual.

Annual Fee to Remain a Consultant: $18

Sales Method: Home parties

Training: Regional training, annual convention, online chat rooms, conference calls, and sponsor training

Online Shop Available? Yes

Commissions: 40% commission on sales

Downline Structure: 3–5% on downline sales

Incentives and Bonuses: Monthly cash bonuses

Inventory: No

Territories: No

Quotas: Must sell $100 retail monthly or $600 every 6 months to remain active

Member of DSA? No

Contact a Representative!

Steph Perez, Independent Sales Consultant. Tel: (760) 373-3591. E-mail: info@passiontoychest.com. Web: www.passiontoychest.com.

Petra Fashions

Petra (pronounced "Paytra") was founded in 1979 by Jonathan and Ingrid Petra Hodges. Petra Fashions specializes in casual and sensual lifestyle apparel and lingerie. Independent Petra Consultants earn 30% commission on sales. New consultants can receive a $600 start-up kit for $1, which includes sample garments, training video, business cards, consultant guide, catalogs, and games booklet. Training is provided through monthly branch meetings, annual events, and upline sponsors.

Company: Petra Fashions, 35 Cherry Hill Drive, Danvers, MA 01923-2594. Tel: 800-738-7248 or 978-777-5853. E-mail: petra@petrafashions.com. Web: www.petrafashions.com.

Products: Lingerie

Years in Business: Since 1979

Countries of Operation: U.S.

Starter Kit/Start-Up Costs: $1 (a $600 value), includes training video, business cards, catalogs, plus garments, consultant guide, and games booklet.

Sales Method: Home parties

Training: Monthly branch meetings, annual events, and upline training

Online Shop Available? No

Commissions: 30% commission on sales

Incentives and Bonuses: Trips, jewelry, bonuses

Inventory: No

Territories: No

Quotas: Quota applies to receive downline commissions; holding 3 shows per months is active status.

Member of DSA? Yes

Contact a Representative in Your Area!

Holly Pavlyik, Director, Gibbstown, NJ. Tel: (856) 308-3117. Fax: (270) 458-1466. E-mail: hollys_petra_fashions@yahoo.com. Web: www.webspawner.com/users/pavlyik/index.html.

Premier Designs Jewelry

Premier Designs sells a line of high fashion jewelry. Premier is in its 19th year of business. Premier Designs Jewelers (Independent Distributors) have two avenues for earning income. Jewelers earn 50% commission on sales, plus 10% commission on the wholesale of team members through three generations down. National Rallies, including motivation, training, and recognition, are available.

Jewelers receive a comprehensive training manual and instruction and guidance from experienced field leaders. They also have available an array of audio and video training tapes and one-on-one service from their customer service representatives. The starter kit is $395, which includes *The Guide to Effective Master Jewelers Manual*, catalogs, 100 order forms, audio tapes, and all necessary paperwork. The annual fee to remain a consultant is $350.

Company: Premier Designs, P.O. Box 619220, Dallas, Texas 75261-9220. (1551 Corporate Drive Irving, Texas 75038-2431.) Tel: 800-486-7378 or 972-550-0955. Fax: 972-580-8222. Web: www.premierdesigns.com.

Products: High fashion jewelry

Years in Business: 19 years

Countries of Operation: U.S.

Starter Kit/Start-Up Costs: $395, which includes policy manual, forms, training tapes.

Annual Fee to Remain a Consultant: $350

Sales Method: Home shows

Training: Monthly

Online Shop Available? No

Commissions: 50% commission on sales

Downline Structure: 10% commission on 1st, 2nd, and 3rd levels

Incentives and Bonuses: Trips, free jewelry

Inventory: No

Territories: No

Quotas: None, except must sell $200/month retail to receive downline commission

Company Accolades: 10% of all company profits are donated to Christian Missions.

Member of DSA? Yes

Contact a Representative in Your Area!

FLORIDA

Sheri L. Ringpfiel, Independent Distributor, Jacksonville, FL. Tel: (904) 998-9021. E-mail: RSRingpfiel@aol.com.

ILLINOIS

Eileen Blackburn, 2-Diamond Designer, O'Fallon, IL. Tel: (618) 628-1830. Fax: (618) 628-1830. E-mail: emblackburn@usa.net. Web: www.premierdesigns.com.

KENTUCKY

Elaine Raque Jetton, Independent Distributor, Louisville, KY. Tel: (502) 456-4283. Fax: (502) 452-6326. E-mail: topjewelry@aol.com.

MISSOURI

Eileen Blackburn, 2-Diamond Designer, O'Fallon, IL. Tel: (618) 628-1830. Fax: (618) 628-1830. E-mail: emblackburn@usa.net. Web: www.premierdesigns.com.

TEXAS

Debra Bennett, Harlingen, TX. Tel: (956) 428-7720.
E-mail: AtHomeDebra@aol.com.

VIRGINIA

Mary Ellen Furman, Amissville, VA. Tel: (540) 347-7578. E-mail: Mefurman2@aol.com.

Princess House

Princess House is a direct selling company specializing in products for the home, including hand blown and lead crystal, tableware, cookware, bakeware, serveware and collectibles. The company operates a distribution center in Rural Hall, North Carolina and a headquarters in Taunton, Massachusetts. Princess house currently has 15,000 Lifestyle Consultants and Organizers in the U.S. and Puerto Rico. Princess House also has bilingual opportunities, as Spanish-speaking Lifestyle Consultants are their fastest-growing segment of consultants. The company has a bilingual corporate staff and translated tools and materials to support these Lifestyle Consultants in starting and growing their own businesses.

There are six levels of independent Princess House business owners, beginning with Lifestyle Consultant and rising to Field Organizer, their highest level of management. Incentives include trips, regional and national awards and recognition, and product discounts. Lifestyle Consultants are supported by corporate marketing, sales and customer service professionals as well as business tools, materials, and training. Princess House was established in 1963 by entrepreneur Charles Collis.

Company: Princess House, 470 Myles Standish Blvd., Taunton, MA 02780. Tel: 800-622-0039 or 508-823-6800. E-mail: custsvc@princesshouse.com. Web: www.princesshouse.com.

Products: Lifestyle and organizing products

Years in Business: Since 1963

Countries of Operation: U.S.

Sales Method: Home parties

Member of DSA? Yes

Contact a Representative!

Donna Waddle Kirkpatrick, Area Organizer, Hartselle, AL. Tel: (256) 773-8558. Fax: (256) 751-4029. E-mail: jhwaddle@msn.com. Web: www.princesshouse.com/consultants/Dwaddle.

Richmont Direct

Founded in 2002, Richmont Direct currently offers four product lines—cooking and entertaining products; Christmas ornaments and décor; jewelry, gifts and collectibles; and Richmont Creations™, a collection of products that can be personalized with a photo or image. Consultants earn up to a 30% commission on all personal sales, and can purchase product samples at a 50% discount. Consultants also earn 6% commission on first-level team members, and an additional 5% commission on the second-level recruits.

Their starter kit is the Success Showcase, which includes sample products from all four product lines (a total of seven items); a three-month, trial subscription to the Richmont Direct Personal Web Page Program; seven catalogs from each product line; a video, "A Conversation with John Rochon," (their founder); literature and forms; the Richmont Consultant Manual; and a silver butterfly pin created by Ross-Simons for new consultants to wear as a conversation-starter for selling and recruiting. The Success Showcase is available for between $74.95–$99, depending on kit special that month (a retail value of $225).

Company: Richmont Direct, P.O. Box 262529, Plano, Texas 75026. (2400 Dallas Parkway; Suite 230, Plano, Texas 75093.) Tel: 866-312-0800 or 972-309-6000. E-mail: customerservice@richmontdirect.com. Web: www.richmont.net

Products: Housewares, gifts, jewelry

Years in Business: Since 2002

Starter Kit/Start-Up Costs: $74.95–$99.95 (retail value $225), includes products, catalogs, training video, literature and forms, and manual

Sales Method: Home parties and direct selling

Commissions: 30% on sales. Samples at 50% off.

Downline Structure: 6% on 1st level and 5% on 2nd level

Inventory: No

Territories: No

Member of DSA? Yes

Contact a Representative in Your Area!

CALIFORNIA

Jeannie Merritt, Manager. Tel: (510) 483-3924. E-mail: LadyRichmont@aol.com. Web: www.richmont.net/ladyrichmont.

NEVADA

Jeannie Merritt, Manager. Tel: (510) 483-3924. E-mail: LadyRichmont@aol.com. Web: www.richmont.net/ladyrichmont.

TEXAS

Shannon Bordelon. E-mail: sbordelon@pobox.com. Web: www.Richmont.net/ Funshopping.

SeneGence International

SeneGence International specializes in waterproof cosmetics. Distributors can purchase products at a 20–50% discount can earn 25%+ commission on sales. SeneGence™ Distributors may sell product via in-home or in-office demonstrations, privately-owned non-chain retail establishments, trade shows, and company-sanctioned Internet and kiosk programs.

They have a variety of start-up options, from $45–$500. The sales packet alone with application deposit is $45 and is refundable upon termination. The New Distributor Kit is $45 (with application deposit waived, but is nonrefundable) and includes the Sales Packet, business supplies, and a training video. The Order Builder Kit is $155, and contains the New Distributor Kit, a product demo video, and business supplies. The SeneCeutical™ Inventory Starter Kit is $500.00 and includes the Complete Starter Kit and pre-selected SeneDerm™ and SeneCosmetic™ inventory for resale. Finally, the Complete Starter Kit is $295 and includes the New Distributor Kit, the Product Demo Kit, the Product Demo Video, and the SeneCeutical™ Product Knowledge CD.

SeneGence's premier product LipSense (liquid lip color) has been in the marketplace since April 1999, with eyeliner, eyebrow, and mascara products debuting by the end of the year 2000.

Company: SeneGence International, Inc., 4000 Birch Street, Suite 112, Newport Beach, CA 92660. Tel: 949-261-3200. Fax: 949-622-8866. E-mail: info@SeneGence.com. Web: www.senegence.com.

Products: Cosmetics

Starter Kit/Start-Up Costs: $45–$500, depending on package

Sales Method: Home demonstrations, trade shows, online kiosks

Training: Manual, upline sponsor

Commissions: 20–50% commission on sales

Inventory: No

Territories: No

Member of DSA? Yes

Contact a Representative in Your Area!

NEW YORK

Robin Friedman. E-mail: robin@senesite.com. Web: www.senegence.com/robin.

OHIO

Barbara Wolfort, Independent Distributor, Moreland Hills, OH. Tel: (440) 498-9983. Fax: (440) 498-9983. E-mail: barbwolfort@aol.com.
Web: www.senegence.com/ohio.

Sensaria

Sensaria Natural Bodycare products were founded more than 20 years ago by a chemist who suffered from severe skin allergies due to the chemicals in skin and body care products. The products are developed using active, natural plant and flower extracts. They are safe for the environment and not tested on animals. Products include skincare, hair care, cleansers, moisturizers, and sun care products. Independent Representatives sell through Sensaria Spa Classes.

Incentives include the opportunity to earn trips and bonuses. No inventory or delivery is required. Training is provided through sponsors, newsletters, training materials, and conference calls. The Business Kit includes samples, catalogs, order forms, web site, e-mail address, online tools, training DVD, training CDs, and training manual. The optional Natural Start Kit includes a variety of full size products to start doing Sensaria Spa Classes. Representatives earn 30% commission, 6–10% personal volume bonuses and 5–12% on downline sales. Customers can order directly from Sensaria and representatives receive full commission.

Company: Sensaria (formerly Natural Bodycare), 3260 East Johns Prairie Road, Suite 1, Shelton, WA 98584-8229. Tel: 360-432-3200. Fax: 360-432-3210. Web: www.sensaria.com.

Products: Skincare (facial cleansers, exfoliants, toners, masks, and moisturizers) and body care (aromatherapy, bubble bath, hand & foot care, sun care, home care, and hair care).

Years in Business: 3 years in direct sales.

Countries of Operation: U.S.

Starter Kit/Start-Up Costs: $115 Business Kit includes samples, catalogs, order forms, web site, e-mail address, online tools, training DVD, training CDs, and training manual. Representatives also have the option to purchase the $115 Natural Start Kit that includes a variety of full size products to start doing Sensaria Spa Classes (retail value: $376.50).

Annual Fee to Remain a Consultant: $60

Sales Method: Home parties

Training: Teleclasses, e-mail updates, team meetings, newsletters, and annual convention

Online Shop Available? Yes

Commissions: 30% commission on sales

Downline Structure: 5–12% on downline sales

Incentives and Bonuses: Sales and recruiting bonuses, monthly bonuses

Inventory: No

Territories: No

Quotas: $75 in monthly personal volume to remain active.

Member of DSA? Yes

Contact a Representative!

Deanna Winn, Meridian, ID. E-mail: deanna@mysensaria.com. Web: www.mysensaria.com/deanna.

Southern Living at HOME

Southern Living at HOME sells home décor and garden items, cooking, garden and idea books, kitchen tools, and food mixes and is connected to the magazine, *Southern Living*. At the end of 2003, there were 31,500 consultants in U.S. The starter kit is $199, which includes $450 worth of product, a supply of catalogs, order forms, consultant manual, and a one-year subscription to *Southern Living* magazine. Consultants earn 25% commission, plus 2–8% overrides on team members. Training is provided through an annual conventions and regional trainings.

Southern Living At HOME is the direct sales company of Southern Progress Corporation, a subsidiary of Time Inc. The corporate headquarters are located in Birmingham, Alabama, while Independent Consultants serve communities throughout the United States. The company was founded in January 2001.

Directors can earn .25%-3% on downline sales through four generations. SLAH's annual convention provides hands-on workshops, free gifts, and in-depth. For incentives, two vacations are offered each year for Consultants to earn through their sales and recruiting efforts. A Director's Retreat is held early in the year, and the General Incentive is held during the summer.

Company: Southern Living at HOME, P.O. Box 830951, Birmingham, AL 35283. Tel: 512-703-8030. E-mail: info@southernlivingathome.com. Web: www.southernlivingathome.com.

Products: Home décor and garden items, cooking & kitchen essentials, books

Years in Business: Since 2001

Countries of Operation: U.S.

Starter Kit/Start-Up Costs: $199, which includes $500 worth of products, catalogs, order forms, training manual, and a one-year subscription to *Southern Living* magazine.

Annual Fee to Remain a Consultant: $25–$50

Sales Method: Home Parties

Training: Annual conventions, regional trainings, e-mail and telephone support

Online Shop Available? Yes

Commissions: 25% commission on sales

Downline Structure: ¼ % to 9% on team member sales as a Director

Incentives and Bonuses: Merchandise and trips

Inventory: No

Territories: No

Quotas: Must sell $500 monthly to remain active and receive overrides

Member of DSA? Yes

Contact a Representative in Your Area!

COLORADO

Alana Weston, Star Director. Tel: (866) 464-7524. Fax: (303) 265-9284. E-mail: alana_weston@hotmail.com. Web: www.southernlivingathome.com/alana.

FLORIDA

Leeanna Fatovic, Star Consultant, Coral Springs, FL. Tel: (954) 336-1390. Fax: (954) 753-5397. E-mail: leeannafatovic@cs.com.
Web: www.southernlivingathome.com/lfatovic.

GEORGIA

Tanya Zingleman, Director, Atlanta, GA. Tel: (770) 889-5733. E-mail: tanya@homesfromtheheart.biz. Web: www.SouthernLivingAtHome.com/Tanya.

INDIANA

Betsy Voigt, Star Consultant, Brownsburg, IN. Tel: (317) 858-1838. E-mail: decoratesouthern@aol.com. Web: www.southernlivingathome.com/Betsy1.

MARYLAND

Kim Davis, Independent Consultant, Silver Spring, MD. Tel: (301) 603-8736. E-mail: mkbklkdavis@msn.com. Web: www.southernlivingathome.com/kimdavis.

NEW JERSEY

Deb Welaish Sutphen, Frenchtown, NJ. Tel: (908) 996-6333. E-mail: drws@earthlink.net. Web: www.southernlivingathome.com/debathome.

OHIO

Elizabeth Weizman, Sales Consultant. Tel: (937) 684-6514. E-mail: ecwitalia@yahoo.com. Web: www.southernlivingathome.com/elizabethw.

PENNSYLVANIA

Karen L. Snyder, Star Director, Doylestown, PA. Tel: (215) 794-7939. Fax: (215) 794-7939. E-mail: athomekaren@comcast.net.
Web: www.southernlivingathome.com/karensnyder.

SOUTH CAROLINA

Darcy Blake. E-mail: SouthernBelle@iglide.net.
Web: www.southernlivingathome.com/southernbelle.

TENNESSEE

Tanya Zingleman, Director, Atlanta, GA. Tel: (770) 889-5733. E-mail: tanya@homesfromtheheart.biz. Web: www.SouthernLivingAtHome.com/Tanya.

TEXAS

Tanya Zingleman, Director, Atlanta, GA. Tel: (770) 889-5733. E-mail: tanya@homesfromtheheart.biz. Web: www.SouthernLivingAtHome.com/Tanya.

WISCONSIN

Joy Vertz, Director. Tel: (262) 268-9588. E-mail: joyv@execpc.com. Web: www.southernlivingathome.com/joyvertz.

Stampin' Up!

Stampin' Up! sells wood-mounted decorative rubber stamps and accessories for use in creating greeting cards and scrapbook pages, as well as home décor and other craft projects. The stamps are sold at home workshops in the U.S. and Canada through a network of nearly 40,000 Demonstrators. Demonstrators earn 20% commission on sales, plus up to an additional 12% based on monthly sales. Downline commissions are between 2–5%. The company has been in business for 16 years.

The standard starter kit is $199 (a retail value of $360), and includes a sampling of rubber stamps, assorted ink pads, card stock, and pastels, accessories, the Demonstrator Manual, the current catalog, introductory videos, getting started information, stampin' techniques brochure, and order forms and business supplies. A larger starter kits is available for $249.

Incentives include cruises and trips, free stamp sets, free catalogs, financial rewards based on sales, annual achievement awards, and a Great Rewards points program. Training is provided through an annual convention, regional seminars, leadership conferences, demonstrator Web site, training videos, and publications.

Stampin' Up! has achieved many awards, including the lists of Utah's Top 15 Revenue Growth and Utah's Top 100 Fastest Growing Companies by MountainWest Venture Group; the Utah Work/Life Award as one of the Top 10 Family-Friendly Companies; and numerous *Creating Keepsakes* Readers' Choice Awards for their rubber stamps and paper collections.

Company: Stampin' Up!, 9350 South 150 East, Fifth Floor, Sandy UT 84070. (in 2005, new address will be: 12695 South 3600 West, Riverton, UT 84065). Tel: 800-STAMPUP. Fax: 801-601-5445. E-mail: ds@stampinup.com. Web: www.stampinup.com.

Products: Decorative rubber stamp sets and accessories for home décor, greeting cards, craft projects, and scrapbooking

Years in Business: 16 years (since 1988)

Countries of Operation: U.S. and Canada

Starter Kit/Start-Up Costs: $199–$249 ($285–$355 CAN), and includes a sampling of Stampin' Up! rubber stamp sets, assorted ink pads, card stock, and pastels in coordinating colors, accessories, Demonstrator Manual, current catalog, two introductory videos, stamping techniques brochure, getting started information, and order forms and business supplies. (Contents are subject to change.) Retail value is $360 ($505 CAN).

Sales Method: Demonstrations

Training: Annual convention, regional seminars, leadership conferences, Demonstrator Web site, training videos and publications

Online Shop Available? Yes

Commissions: 20% commission on sales, with an additional 12% available based on monthly sales

Downline Structure: 5%-10% on downline sales

Incentives and Bonuses: Cruises and trips, free stamp sets, free catalogs, financial rewards based on sales, annual achievement awards, and a Great Rewards points program

Inventory: No

Territories: No

Quotas: Must sell $300 net sales every quarter to remain active.

Company Accolades: Stampin' Up! has achieved many awards, including the lists of Utah's Top 15 Revenue Growth and Utah's Top 100 Fastest Growing Companies by MountainWest Venture Group; the Utah Work/Life Award as one of the Top 10 Family-Friendly Companies; and numerous *Creating Keepsakes* Readers' Choice Awards for their rubber stamps and paper collections.

Member of DSA? Yes

Contact a Representative in Your Area!

COLORADO

Judy Nicholson, Independent Demonstrator, Littleton, CO. Tel: (303) 708-9347. E-mail: franknjudy@msn.com.

FLORIDA

Cathy Caprio. Tel: (954) 566-5620. Fax: (954) 564-2638. E-mail: Credo17537@aol.com. Web:

ILLINOIS

Lisa Kuntz, Independent Demonstrator/Senior Manager, Prospect Heights, IL. Tel: (847) 506-1223. E-mail: stampwithlisa@comcast.net. Web: www.lisak.stampinup.net.

KANSAS

Mimi Henwood, Olathe, KS. Tel: (913) 390-6899. E-mail: stampin@mimistamps.com. Web: www.mimi.stampinup.net.

KENTUCKY

Laureen Shefchik, Executive, Union, KY. E-mail: GeeStamp@insightbb.com. Web: www.StampLadyKY.stampinup.net.

MICHIGAN

Jackie Bolhuis, Zeeland, MI. Tel: (616) 875-3011. E-mail: jbolhuis@chartermi.net. Web: www.jackiebolhuis.stampinup.net.

MINNESOTA

Kristin Engbrecht, Manager, Rochester, MN. Tel: (507) 288-5824. E-mail: kwamengbrecht@netzero.net. Web: www.kengbrecht.stampinup.net.

MISSOURI

Mimi Henwood, Olathe, KS. Tel: (913) 390-6899. E-mail: stampin@mimistamps.com. Web: www.mimi.stampinup.net.

NEW MEXICO

Tammy K. Fite, Senior Manager, Albuquerque, NM. Tel: (505) 899-4935. E-mail: stampinmama@comcast.net. Web: www.tammyfite.stampinup.net.

NORTH CAROLINA

Carolyn Bosley, Independent Demonstrator, Lansing, NC. Tel: (336) 982-9324. E-mail: cbosley@skybest.com.

OHIO

Sharon Duvelius, Executive Director, Fairfield Twp., OH. Tel: (513) 737-5517. E-mail: sduvelius@cinci.rr.com. Web: www.sharonduvelius.stampinup.net.

PENNSYLVANIA

Judy Bickel, Supervisor, Northumberland, PA. Tel: (570) 473-7244. E-mail: jbickel@ptd.net. Web: www.judysstampin.stampinup.net.

TENNESSEE

Susan VanOrman, Memphis, TN. Tel: (901) 624-4949. E-mail: suzystampr@aol.com. Web: http://susanvanorman.stampinup.net.

TEXAS

Kathy Rocco, Senior Executive, Austin, TX. Tel: (512) 328-0272. Fax: (512) 328-5032. E-mail: KathyRocco@aol.com. Web: www.kathy.stampinup.net.

VIRGINIA

C. Adams, Independent Stampin' Up! Demonstrator. E-mail: CraftinMemories@yahoo.com. Web: http://CraftinMemories.stampinup.net.

WASHINGTON

Karen Gregorian, Executive/Demonstrator, Spokane, WA. Tel: (509) 999-9514. Fax: (509) 892-0913. E-mail: stampwithme@yahoo.com.

WEST VIRGINIA

Leann Smith, Sr. Manager Demonstrator, Mineral Wells, WV. Tel: (304) 489-3237. Fax: (304) 489-3237. E-mail: Llasmith67@aol.com.

Top Line Creations

Top Line Creations, 3759 West 2340 South, Suite D, Salt Lake City, Utah 84120. Tel: 866-954-0559 or 801-954-0559. Fax: 801-954-0370. Email: info@topline-creations.com. Web: www.topline-creations.com.

Top Line Creations (TLC) sells scrapbooking supplies such as post-bound, top-loading albums, 3-ring binder albums, album refills, adhesives, page kits, tags, mini tags, letter stickers, die cuts, mini frames, vellum, phrase stickers, and more. The company has been in business approximately 2 years as Top Line Creations (previously known as Cock-a-Doodle Designs). There are approximately 3,000 consultants in the U.S. and Canada.

TLC consultants earn 25–45% commission on sales, plus 5–10% on downline sales. The starter kit is $100 and includes one Total LapTop Crop Bag, catalogs, marketing folders, six page element kits, order forms, applications and agreements, three collective elements bags, two 12x12 storyline pages, two 4x6 lifeline cards, two 50% coupons, and a consultant CD.

Company: Top Line Creations, 3759 West 2340 South, Suite D, SLC, Utah 84120. Tel: 866-954-0559 or 801-954-0559. Fax: 801-954-0370. Email: info@topline-creations.com. Web: www.topline-creations.com.

Products: Scrapbooking supplies

Years in Business: 2 years

Countries of Operation: U.S. and Canada

Starter Kit/Start-Up Costs: Starter kit costs $100 (a retail value of more than $300) and contains one Total LapTop Crop Bag, catalogs, marketing folders, six page element kits, order forms, applications and agreements, three collective elements bags, two 12x12 storyline pages, 2 4x6 lifeline cards, two 50% coupons, and a consultant CD.

Sales Method: Home parties, crops, online, catalog sales, direct selling

Training: Yearly convention, regional and area meetings, online and phone training

Online Shop Available? Yes

Commissions: 25–45% commission on sales

Downline Structure: 5–10% downline commission

Incentives and Bonuses: Top Line Cash earned on all orders over $150. Incentive points can be earned towards trips and convention costs. Directors earn additional commission on downline, based on sales volume.

Inventory: No

Territories: No

Quotas: Only required to receive downline commissions

Member of DSA? Yes

Contact a Representative!

Jan Pepe, Georgia. E-mail: scrap3mom@aol.com. Web:

The Traveling Vineyard

The Traveling Vineyard is a wine tasting party plan company, set up to make customers more confident in selecting wine and in the process, increasing customers' appreciation and enjoyment of fine wine. Their wines come from all over the world, including Napa Valley and Sonoma County from California, Hunter Valley in Australia, The Bordeaux region in France, Tuscany in Italy, plus wines from South Africa, South America, Spain, and the Pacific Northwest.

The Traveling Vineyard does business only in the U.S., and has 500 Independent Personal Wine Consultants in 26 states. Their home parties are called "Wine Tastings" or "In-Home Wine Adventures." To remain active, consultants must have at least two home parties within a 60 day period. They can legally support consultants in Alaska, Arizona, California, Connecticut, Colorado, Florida, Illinois, Iowa, Louisiana, Massachusetts, Michigan, Minnesota, Missouri, North Carolina, North Dakota, Nebraska, New Hampshire, New Jersey, Nevada, New York, Ohio, Oregon, Virginia, Washington, and West Virginia (double-check with company for your state).

Company The Traveling Vineyard, 960 Turnpike Street, Canton, MA 02021. Tel: 866-547-9463. Fax: 800-329-8466. E-mail: info@thetravelingvineyard.com. Web: www.thetravelingvineyard.com.

Products: Wine

Years in Business: The main company has been in business for 18 years, the home party business has been in operation a few months.

Countries of Operation: U.S.

Starter Kit/Start-Up Costs: Starter kit is $250 and contains more than $400 worth of accessories, wine glasses, a manual, wine course, video, brochures, and all items necessary to do wine parties.

Sales Method: Home parties.

Training: Continuous training available online, through monthly meetings, newsletters, message boards, and telephone conferences.

Online Shop Available? No

Commissions: 20% on all wines, accessories, and personal purchases

Downline Structure: Senior Consultants and above earn between 2–5% on downline recruits.

Incentives and Bonuses: Monthly marketing and recruiting contests, promotion and recognition bonuses, and incentive trips.

Inventory: No. A sample set of 6 wines are needed when booking a party.

Territories: No territories, but consultants can only offer parties and have wine shipped to states that allow direct shipment of wine across state lines.

Quotas: To remain active, consultants must have two home parties in a 60 day period.

Company Accolades: In a 12 month period, they have increased sales exceeding 500%.

Member of DSA? Yes

Contact a Representative!

Kym McDowell, Unlimited Enterprises, Wine Consultant, Houston, TX. Tel: (281) 359-1022. Fax: (281) 358-8344. E-mail: wineparty@wine-tasting-parties.com. Web: www.wine-tasting-parties.com.

Tupperware

Perhaps the most well-known party-plan company, Tupperware has been in business for 54 years. They sell kitchen products and gadgets, most well-known for their invention of the self-sealing "burp" of the plastic Tupperware container. Consultants sell mainly through home parties, and earn between 25–35% commission on sales. Commissions on team members range from 3–5%. The starter kit includes $100 worth of products and approximately $25 in business supplies, all of which costs $63.

Company: Tupperware Corporation, P.O. Box 2353, Orlando, FL 32802. Tel: 800-366-3800. Web: http://my.tupperware.com.

Products: Tupperware products and housewares

Years in Business: 54 years

Countries of Operation: 100 countries

Starter Kit/Start-Up Costs: $63, includes $100 worth of products and business supplies

Annual Fee to Remain a Consultant: None

Sales Method: Home parties

Training: Video training, weekly training

Online Shop Available? Yes

Commissions: 25–35% commission on sales

Downline Structure: 3–5% commission on downline sales

Incentives and Bonuses: Free products, trips, company car program

Inventory: No

Territories: No

Quotas: Must sell $50/month retail to remain active

Company Accolades: Tupperware named as one of the top 100 inventions of the 20th century

Member of DSA? Yes

Contact a Representative in Your Area!

CALIFORNIA

Linda Weinstein, Manager. E-mail: lweinstein@my.tupperware.com. Web:

IDAHO

Kim Ross, Manager, Boise, ID. Tel: (208) 433-9949.
E-mail: kimross@my.tupperware.com. Web: www.my.tupperware.com/KimRoss.

ILLINOIS

Pat Kopicki, Tupperware Manager. Tel: (708) 354-0995.
Email: iselltupperware2@aol.com. Web: www.my.tupperware.com/pkopicki.

INDIANA

Debby Dodd, VIP Manager, Southport, IN. Tel: (317) 786-2501.
E-mail: diamonddodd@my.tupperware.com.
Web: my.tupperware.com/diamonddodd.com.

UTAH

Spencer White. Tel: (801) 371-2761. E-mail: whitefamily@my.tupperware.com.
Web: http://my.tupperware.com/whitefamily.

UBB's Natural Family Boutique

UBB's Natural Family Boutique (formerly Unique Baby Boutique) was founded in 2002 by Kim Pekin, a breastfeeding advocate and mother committed to attachment parenting. Her company is dedicated to providing attachment parenting, breastfeeding, and natural childbirth products. Product categories include pregnancy; labor and birth; postpartum; breastfeeding; mommy pampering; natural baby care; cloth diapering; organic baby clothing; wooden toys; non-toxic art products; baby slings; natural birth and parenting books and videos; belly casting/hand and foot casting kits; organic bedding; beeswax candles; Holly Lane Designs Jewelry, and more.

UBB Sales Consultants earn 25% commission on sales, plus 2–3% on team members. Commission can rise as high as 40% with downline sales and bonuses. The UBB Mini Kit is $99 (a retail value of more than $165) and contains 6 product samples, catalogs, order forms, and binder. The UBB Basic Kit is $249 (a retail value of more than $400) and contains 13 best-selling products, business supplies, catalogs, brochures, invitations, business cards, fabric swatches, hostess packet, recruit packet, order forms, and binder. There is also a Doula Business Start-Up Kit for $169 (retail value of $500) containing 10 natural childbirth product samples, business supplies, catalogs, order forms, and binder. With a 50% down payment, consultants can pay for the starter kit over a two-month period.

UBB's products are breastfeeding friendly and don't contain images of bottles or pacifiers used as decoration on any of their products. Whenever possible, their products are made with either organic or natural materials, or they provide some environmental benefit. Reps earn a commission of 25% of the total Sales Value (Sales Value is the wholesale price, 80% of retail price). There are currently approximately 250 UBB reps.

Company: Unique Natural Family Boutique, 17232 Pickwick Drive, Purcellville, VA 20132-3100. Tel: 866-672-7843 or 540-338-0330. Fax: 703-783-0511E-mail: webmaster@uniquebabyboutique.com. Web: www.uniquebabyboutique.com.

Products: Attachment parenting and natural childbirth products

Years in Business: Since 2002

Countries of Operation: U.S.

Starter Kit/Start-Up Costs: $99 for the MiniKit (retail value $165), which includes 6 products, business supplies, catalogs, order forms, and binder. $249

for the Basic Kit (retail value $400), which includes 13 products, business supplies, catalogs, order forms, binder, fabric swatches, recruiting and hostess packets, opportunity brochures, hostess brochures, invitations, and business cards. There is also a Doula Start-Up Kit for $169 (retail value $500) and contains 10 natural childbirth products, plus business supplies. A payment plan is available.

Sales Method: Home parties, direct selling, online, and fundraisers

Training: Upline sponsors, online training groups

Online Shop Available? Yes

Commissions: 25–40% commission on sales

Downline Structure: Up to 3%, depending on Consultant level achieved and recruit generation (1st, 2nd, 3rd, etc.)

Incentives and Bonuses: Great Expectations program that awards free business builder kits, increases in rank and commissions, free products, and a $249 rebate for the Basic Demo Kit.

Inventory: No

Territories: No

Quotas: Must sell $100 per quarter to remain active.

Member of DSA? Yes

Contact a Representative in Your Area!

FLORIDA

Heather Womersley, Sales Consultant, St. Petersburg, FL. Tel: (727) 580-3529. Fax: (727) 531-0006.E-mail: hwomersley@yahoo.com.
Web: www.uniquebabyboutique.com/?HMWom.

MICHIGAN

Jean Jones, Associate Sales Team Leader. Tel: (269) 672-5992.
E-mail: jonesfamily@netpenny.net. Web: www.ShopUBB.com/?jeanjones.

VIRGINIA

Darlene White, Sales Team Coordinator. E-mail: wfamof6@iglide.net.

USANA Health Sciences

USANA offers health products, including Usana Essentials (vitamins), Optimizers (nutritional products), and Macro-Optimizers (macro-nutrients). Independent Associate commissions vary based on a complex multi-level recruit system. Starter kits range from $250 to $1,250 and contain a variety of products, training materials, and marketing materials, depending on kit purchased. Training is available online, through conference calls, regional and national conferences, and conventions. Reps earn between 10–20% commission on sales, plus 10–20% on downline sales.

USANA operates in the U.S., Canada, Australia, Mexico, Singapore, Hong Kong, Japan, and others. Their mission is to "develop and provide the highest quality, science-based health products, distributed internationally through network marketing."

USANA began operations in September of 1992. USANA's Medical Advisory Board, on-staff Ph.D.s, physicians, and distributors include many highly respected business and health care leaders. USANA's Business Plan is designed to pay commissions on sales volume, with no limit to the number of levels from which you can earn weekly commissions.

Company: USANA Health Sciences, 3838 West Parkway Blvd., Salt Lake City, UT 84120. Tel: 801-954-7200. Fax: 801-954-7300. E-mail: distserv@usana.com. Web: www.usana.com.

Products: Vitamins, nutritional products, and macro-nutrients

Years in Business: Since 1992

Countries of Operation: 12 countries, including U.S., Canada, Australia, Mexico, Singapore, Hong Kong, and Japan

Starter Kit/Start-Up Costs: Starter kits range from $250–$1,250 and contain a variety of products, training materials, and marketing materials, depending on kit purchased.

Annual Fee to Remain a Consultant: $20

Sales Method: Direct selling, online

Training: Online training, conference calls, local/regional conferences and conventions

Online Shop Available? Yes

Commissions: 10–20%

Downline Structure: 10–20%

Incentives and Bonuses: Compensation plan

Inventory: No

Territories: No

Quotas: No

Member of DSA? Yes

Contact a Representative!

Marion Carrithers, Louisville, KY. Tel: (502) 458-4265. Fax: (502) 451-9299. E-mail: mcarrithers@earthlink.net. Web: www.usanasuccess.com

Usborne Books at Home

Usborne Books at Home (UBAH) is the home business division of Educational Development Corporation (EDC), recently named as one of *Fortune* magazine's top 100 fastest growing companies (*Fortune Small Business*, July/Aug 2003). EDC began this home business division in March 1989, and was the first multilevel direct selling company in the United States to offer primarily nonfiction educational books for children. Usborne Books at Home markets the entire Usborne line of more than 1,000 titles through a combination of direct sales, home parties, fundraisers, and book fairs. Their independent sales consultants are selling books in all 50 states and number approximately 10,000 in the U.S.

Usborne books are fascinating, lavishly illustrated books written with humor, surprise, and drama. They incorporate activities and puzzles to challenge a child's observation and intelligence. Their printing quality and well-produced graphics, high ratio of pictures to text, short magazine-like format, and unique detail set Usborne books apart from other books. There is a wide range of subjects covering hobbies, science, nature, parent's guides and more. Usborne books truly appeal to all ages, infants to adults. Usborne's unique features include: 1) Step-by-step explanations of the "How's and Why's;" 2) Cutaway illustrations so children can get the inside view; 3) Double page layouts which open so that the book is easily propped up; 4) Pages filled with activity; 5) Straightforward text consistently positioned below each picture simplifying the reading exercise; and 6) Many of Usborne's preschool books feature charming illustrations by Stephen Cartwright with a "find the duck" theme throughout. Their representatives are called "Educational Consultants," and their home party is home show.

Company: Usborne Books at Home, A Division of Educational Development Corporation, 10302 E. 55th Place, Tulsa, OK 74146-6515. Tel: 800-611-1655. Fax: 918-663-2525. E-mail: edc@edcpub.com or ubah@ubah.com. Web: www.ubah.com.

Products: Nonfiction educational, fun books for children from infant to teenager.

Years in Business: 15

Countries of Operation: U.S.

Starter Kit/Start-Up Costs: The Base Kit includes approximately 30 books, as well as a selection of catalogs, order forms, customer surveys, flyers and the

UBAH Handbook. Cost: $25–$125 (retail value: $50–$220). Special kits are available and change every two months.

Annual Fee to Remain a Consultant: None

Sales Method: A combination of direct sales, home shows, school and library sales, and book fairs.

Training: Local and regional training meetings, plus a National Convention.

Online Shop Available? Yes

Commissions: Home Shows—25%. Direct Sales—15–30%. Book Fairs—17–20%. School and Library Sales—17–25%.

Downline Structure: 1–11% commission on downline sales, plus a 4% recruiting bonus

Incentives and Bonuses: Recruiting bonuses, incentive travel, sales bonuses, and contests.

Inventory: No

Territories: No

Quotas: Must sell $350 in net sales every three months to remain active.

Company Accolades: Named *Forbes* 200 Best Small Companies in America; *Fortune* 100 Fastest Growing Small Companies; and #1 Performing Public Company in Oklahoma.

Member of DSA? Yes.

Contact a Representative in Your Area!

CALIFORNIA

Karen Bolthausen, Educational Consultant, Fullerton, CA. Tel: (714) 526-6376. Fax: (775) 703-2442. E-mail: msbolty@hotmail.com.
Web: www.BooksKidsLove2Read.com.

GEORGIA

Cathy Eads, Supervisor, Duluth, GA. Tel: (888) 305-2120. Fax: (801) 340-2100. E-mail: cathy@findtheduck.com. Web: www.FindTheDuck.com.

ILLINOIS

Chandelle Brink, Independent Educational Consultant, Belleville, IL. Tel: (618) 277-1994. E-mail: skybrink@iglide.net. Web: www.funbook4you.com.

INDIANA

Susan Anderson, Supervisor, Bloomington, IN. Tel: (866) 849-6876. E-mail: Susan4Usborne@cs.com. Web: www.BuyUsborneBooks.com.

IOWA

Wendy Kennedy, Independent Educational Supervisor, Corydon, IN. Tel: (812) 952-1643. E-mail: rwkennedy@insightbb.com. Web: www.Usborne4You.com.

KENTUCKY

Elizabeth Ray, Independent Educational Supervisor, Crestwood, KY. Tel: (502) 243-2285. E-mail: ebeth_ray@yahoo.com. Web: www.WorldofUsborne.com.

MICHIGAN

Cindy Porter-Zidel, Independent Educational Supervisor, Grand Blanc, MI. Tel: (866) 242-5712. E-mail: UsborneCindy@aol.com.
Web: www.UsborneBooksMI.com.

MINNESOTA

Nadette Waligora, Independent Educational Consultant, Isanti, MN. Tel: (866) 351-2485. Fax: (763) 444-6189. E-mail: Nadette@UsborneWorld.com. Web: www.UsborneWorld.com.

MISSOURI

Chris Taylor, Independent Educational Supervisor, St. Peters, MO. Tel: (636) 936-2399. E-mail: christaylorubah@peoplepc.com. Web: www.Usborne4Books.com.

OKLAHOMA

Jolene & Jim Evans, Independent Educational Supervisors, Nash, OK. Tel: (580) 839-2383. E-mail: jolenelovesbooks@yahoo.com.
Web: www.shopusbornebooks.com.

PENNSYLVANIA

Kathy Hughes, Independent Educational Consultant/Supervisor, Whitehall, PA. Tel: (877) 875-1626. E-mail: kdhughes@ptd.net.
Web: www.TheUsborneBookstore.com.

SOUTH CAROLINA

Amy Coquillard, Independent Educational Supervisor, Columbia, SC. Tel: (803) 790-7901. Fax: (877) 345-4985. E-mail: coquillard@yahoo.com. Web: www.amysusbornebooks.com.

TENNESSEE

Cynthia Bothwell, Supervisor, Memphis, TN. Tel: (901) 266-4778. E-mail: ubah4all@aol.com. Web: www.duckbookbiz.com.

UTAH

Shauna Zollinger, Supervisor, Orem, UT. Tel: (801) 426-9923. E-mail: usborne@firston.com. Web: www.ubah.com/k0567.

VitaCorp International

Vitacorp offers a line of vitamins, minerals, herbals, botanicals, enzymes and homeopathics. The cost for enrolling as an affiliate is $29, which includes a personalized Web site, group management tools, web-based resources, and twelve months of business support. The annual renewal fee of $10 is waived for affiliates who have earned at least $100 in bonuses during the previous calendar year.

Company: Vitacorp International, 13100 Northwest Fwy, Suite 440, Houston, TX 77040. Tel: 281-220-1240. Fax: 832-201-7517. E-mail: questions@vitacorp.com. Web: www.vitacorp.com.

Products: Vitamins, minerals, herbals, botanicals, enzymes and homeopathics

Years in Business: 2 years

Countries of Operation: U.S., Canada, UK

Starter Kit/Start-Up Costs: $29, includes Web site

Annual Fee to Remain a Consultant: $10, which is waived for affiliates who've earned $100 in bonuses in the last year.

Sales Method: Direct selling, online

Training: Consultant manual

Online Shop Available? Yes

Incentives and Bonuses: Incentive trips

Inventory: No

Territories: No

Quotas: No

Member of DSA? No

Contact a Representative in Your Area!

TEXAS

Leona L. Schroeder, Houston, TX. Tel: (713) 541-3130. E-mail: lschroeder77024@yahoo.com. Web: http://Leona.TheFunDiet.com.

KANSAS

Gail L. Foley, Witchita, KS. Tel: (316) 831-0203. E-mail: Gail@PassOnASmile.com. Web: www.VitaCorp.com/715712.

Warm Spirit

Warm Spirit sells a line of bath and body products, including:

- **Essentials** (soaps, cleansers, toners; creams, balms, lotions; healthy hair; masks and body treatments; vitamins and supplements)
- **Pleasures** (body butters; massage, body and bath; gift pillows and sachets; therapeutic pillows; and herbal teas)
- **Remedies** (homeopathic formulas and herbal remedies to ease things from backache to PMS to diet support to sore throat.). Their entire product line totals 100 products.

The Basic Kit is $99 and includes product samples, literature and business tools, and paperwork, a retail value of $175. Optional product kits to add on to your basic kit are available, ranging from $200–$500. Consultants earn 25% personal sales commission. Consultants earn gift certificates for new recruits.

An interest in natural products and herbal remedies, as well its tradition of using herbal and homeopathic remedies, is what leads the company's goal toward well being, self care, pampering and nurturing. Their home parties are called "Gatherings," and can revolve around monthly themes, from New Year's to Christmas. They also have monthly product promotions. Consultants have access to 15% commission on sales, weekly training calls, gift certificates for referring new active consultants, and are eligible for their Consultant Online Assistant Program (COLA) and their own Warm Spirit home page.

Company: Warm Spirit, Inc., Field Services Department, 15645 SE 114th Avenue, Suite 202, Clackamas, OR 97015. Tel: 888-296-9854.
E-mail: fieldsupport@warmspirit.com. Web: www.warmspirit.com.

Products: Products: Essentials (Soaps, cleansers, toners; creams, balms, lotions; healthy hair; masks and body treatments; vitamins and supplements); Pleasures (Body Butters; Massage, Body and Bath; Gift Pillows and Sachets; Therapeutic Pillows; and Herbal Teas); Remedies (Homeopathic formulas and Herbal remedies to ease things from backache to PMS to diet support to sore throat).

Years in Business: 5 years

Countries of Operation: U.S.

Starter Kit/Start-Up Costs: The Basic Kit is $99 and includes product samples, literature and business tools, and paperwork, a retail value of $175. Optional product kits to add on to your basic kit are available, ranging from $200–$500.

Sales Method: Gatherings (home parties)

Training: Weekly empowerment conference calls, upline training, home office training

Online Shop Available? Yes

Commissions: 15% commission on sales

Downline Structure: Gift certificates for new active recruits

Incentives and Bonuses: Sales bonuses, prizes, awards, gift certificates, leadership clubs

Inventory: No

Territories: No

Quotas: Applies to active status

Member of DSA? Yes

Contact a Representative in Your Area!

CALIFORNIA

Nicole Deggins, Independent Warm Spirit Consultant #692, Jackson, MS. Toll-free: 877-400-1581. Tel: (504) 329-4839. E-mail: Nicole@WarmSpirit.org. Web: www.warmspirit.org/southernspirit692.

CONNECTICUT

Sherry Fields, Self-Care Consultant. Tel: (888) 239-0041. Fax: (888) 239-0041. E-mail: sherry@warmspirit.org. Web: www.warmspirit.org/sherry.

FLORIDA

Sherry Fields, Self-Care Consultant. Tel: (888) 239-0041. Fax: (888) 239-0041. E-mail: sherry@warmspirit.org. Web: www.warmspirit.org/sherry.

ILLINOIS

Rhonda Adams, Director, Chicago, IL. Tel: (312) 735-1806. E-mail: rhonda@warmspirit.org. Web: www.warmspirit.org/radams.

LOUISIANA

Maxine Henry, Independent Consultant, New Orleans, LA. Tel: (504) 947-0010. E-mail: warmspirit4626@yahoo.com.

MASSACHUSETTS

Kathy Russ, Independent Consultant, Boston, MA. Tel: (617) 256-8187. E-mail: kathy@warmspirit.org. Web: www.warmspirit.org/kathy.

MICHIGAN

Mardi Woods, Director/Independent Consultant. Tel: (313) 510-9242. E-mail: mardiw007@yahoo.com. Web: www.warmspirit.eurekaproducts.org.

MISSISSIPPI

Nicole Deggins, Independent Warm Spirit Consultant #692, Jackson, MS. Toll-free: 877-400-1581. Tel: (504) 329-4839. E-mail: Nicole@WarmSpirit.org. Web: www.warmspirit.org/southernspirit692.

NEW JERSEY

Bernice L. Clark, Independent Self-Care Consultant, Lindenwold, NJ. Tel: (267) 971-0470. Fax: (856) 627-5458. E-mail: bclark@warmspirit.org. Web: www.warmspirit.org/serenespace.

OHIO

Deborah S. Johnson, Associate Manager. Tel: (216) 392-0536. Fax: (216) 692-3745. E-mail: totalcare@ameritech.net. Web: www.warmspirit.org/debjohnson.

PENNSYLVANIA

Maria J. Phelts, Self-Care Consultant, Philadelphia, PA. Tel: (215) 888-6355. E-mail: mphelts@warmspirit.org. Web: www.warmspirit.org/mariaphelts.

Wildtree Herbs, Inc.

Wildtree Herbs Inc. is a new direct-sales company whose gourmet culinary blends, infused oils, dressings and sauces are sold through home parties. Their Independent Representatives show guests how to make cooking a quicker, easier and more healthful project for those who are short on time, and a fun, interesting adventure for those who wish to be more creative in the kitchen.

Wildtree Herbs was established as a small craft/hobby business several years ago by Leslie Montie. Leslie was a typical mother of two young children until both of those children were diagnosed with medical conditions that required special diets. That's when Leslie called her parents, Judy and Frank for help in preparing food for their grandchildren. They started blending herbs and spices tailored from old family recipes. Leslie began to get requests for the blends so she decided to start selling them locally.

Wildtree Herbs' unique herb and spice blends and mixes help families make healthful meals that taste great, are quick and easy to prepare and do not have the hydrogenated fats, preservatives, artificial flavors, or additives in store-bought packaged foods. Their products are free of preservatives, added MSG, fillers, and anti-caking agents. The company also provides recipes to use with their products.

Company: Wildtree Herbs, Inc., 11 Knight Street, Warwick, Rhode Island 02886. Tel: 800-672-4050 or 401-732-1856. Fax: 401-732-1968. E-mail: repinfo@wildtreeherbs.com. Web: www.wildtreeherbs.com.

Products: Infused oils, dressings, sauces, dips, marinades

Years in Business: Since 1996

Countries of Operation: U.S.

Starter Kit/Start-Up Costs: The starter kit is $100 and includes business supplies, training materials, bulk products, top selling oils, dips, seasonings, and sauces. Starter kit enhancements are available. The kit can be earned for free.

Annual Fee to Remain a Consultant: $25

Sales Method: Home parties

Training: DVD and training manual

Online Shop Available? No

Commissions: 25% commission on sales

Downline Structure: Personal Sales Bonus of 3–15%. Team Sales Bonus of 3–15%. Recruiting Bonus of 4%.

Incentives and Bonuses: Monthly sales incentives, annual incentive trip

Inventory: No

Territories: No

Quotas: Yes

Member of DSA? Yes

Contact a Representative in Your Area!

CONNECTICUT

Rosemary Parisi, Team Director, Warwick, RI. Tel: (401) 781-1553. E-mail: herbnspice@cox.net.

MASSACHUSETTS

Monique Simard, Team Leader, Blackstone, MA. Tel: (508) 883-2693. E-mail: moniqueforherbs@comcast.net.

NEW JERSEY

Amy Nelson, Team Leader, Hopatcong, NJ. Tel: (973) 632-8506. E-mail: tinytot018@netscape.net. Web: www.amysparties.biz.

NEW YORK

Rosemary Parisi, Team Director, Warwick, RI. Tel: (401) 781-1553. E-mail: herbnspice@cox.net.

OHIO

Rosemary Parisi, Team Director, Warwick, RI. Tel: (401) 781-1553. E-mail: herbnspice@cox.net.

PENNSYLVANIA

Rosemary Parisi, Team Director, Warwick, RI. Tel: (401) 781-1553. E-mail: herbnspice@cox.net.

RHODE ISLAND

Rosemary Parisi, Team Director, Warwick, RI. Tel: (401) 781-1553. E-mail: herbnspice@cox.net.

Zedora, Inc. (formerly Manuel.Zed)

Zedora, Inc. specializes in the company's collection of Italian charms for bracelets is inspired by Artisan Manuel Zoppini's passion for detailed design, style, and a desire to "merge classical fashion with contemporary expression." The Manuel.Zed bracelets are made up of interlocking charms made of stainless steel in a wide variety of images. Since their name change from Manuel.Zed to Zedora, the company has now broadened their product selection to carry a variety of jewelry pieces and leather accessories. Consultants earn 35% commission, 2% on team members through three levels as well as infinity bonuses. The starter kit is $99 and includes business cards, brochures, a training manual, and consultant packets. Larger kits with jewelry cost up to $2,000. The company currently has 1,400 consultants nationwide.

Their products are manufactured in their privately owned factories in Florence, Italy. All of their charms are stamped on the back with the MANUEL.ZED™ name. Their modular collection is designed to allow its wearer to interchange links at will, therefore creating for themselves the look and feel they desire. In addition to the inclusion of 18K gold and stainless steel, they incorporate enamel, semi-precious and precious stones, and crystals into their products. The bracelets cater to all age groups and genders. In addition to being worn as a bracelet, the Piccolo Collection is commonly used as an anklet because of its thin size and delicate nature. Since stainless steel is virtually maintenance free, a soft cloth is sufficient for cleaning.

Company: Zedora, Inc., 110 East Broward Blvd., Suite 1910, Fort Lauderdale, FL 33301. Tel: 954-332-3322. Fax: 954-332-0028. Web: www.zedora.com.

Products: Charm jewelry

Years in Business: 3 years

Starter Kit/Start-Up Costs: $99–$2,000, including business cards, brochures, training manual, consultant packets and jewelry

Sales Method: Home parties

Training: Training manual, regional events, weekly conference calls, business resource center, Web tools, leadership training/mentoring, a full-time field development trainer

Online Shop Available? Yes

Commissions: 35% commission on sales

Downline Structure: 2% commission of retail sales through four levels

Incentives and Bonuses: Infinity bonuses, business builder bonuses, and matching bonuses

Inventory: No

Territories: No

Quotas: Must purchase a minimum of $20 over 3 months to remain active

Member of DSA? No

Contact a Representative in Your Area!

ARIZONA

Jamie Weber, Owner, Jamie's Jewels, Phoenix, AZ. Tel: (602) 570-4738. E-mail: Jamiesweber@yahoo.com. Web: www.zed.us/2499.

CALIFORNIA

Debra Gallaher and Katherine DeFreitas, Two Charming Ladies, Caruthers, CA, Tel: (559) 864-3071. E-mail: debbie@caruthersraisin.com. Web: www.zed.us/1502.

COLORADO

Cheryl Villaret, Independent Sales Consultant, San Antonio, TX. Tel: (210) 363-1225. E-mail: charmlady@earthlink.net. Web: www.zed.us/2098.

CONNECTICUT

Lisa Gallagher, Charming Creations by Lisa, Connecticut. Tel: (203) 364-0105. E-mail: lggourmet@charter.net.

DELAWARE

Donna Pantaleo and Christy Bohatiuk, Newark, DE. Tel: (302) 239-2386. Fax: (302) 234-4021. E-mail: acharmingdesign@aol.com. Web: www.zed.us/2096.

FLORIDA

Deborah Vincent, Independent Jewelry Consultant. Tel: (707) 451-7560. E-mail: CharmedPleasures@aol.com. Web: www.zed.us/CharmedPleasures.

ILLINOIS

Jane Carhart, Independent Sales Consultant, Minooka, IL. Tel: (815) 509-6222. Fax: (815) 467-2943. E-mail: charms@uti.com. Web: www.zed.us/2013.

INDIANA

Terri Stulgate, Gold Consultant, Schererville, IN. Tel: (219) 365-1911. Fax: (219) 465-4546. E-mail: mz@charmingtreasures.net. Web: www.zed.us/charmingtreasures

MARYLAND

Barbara Efantis, Gold Consultant, Silver Spring, MD. Tel: (301) 593-8432. E-mail: befantis@attg.nt. Web: www.zed.us/1143.

MASSACHUSETTS

Gail Sprenger. E-mail: gaillou@adelphia.net. Web: www.zed.us/2569.

MICHIGAN

Jackie Bolhuis, Zeeland, MI. Tel: (616) 875-3011. E-mail: jbolhuis@chartermi.net.

MINNESOTA

Lori Laliberte, Independent Sales Consultant, Hibbing, MN. Tel: (218) 263-3635. E-mail: lacharm@rangebroadband.com. Web: www.zed.us/1636.

MISSOURI

Amber Munson, Charmed I'm Sure!, Joplin, MO. Tel: (417) 483-7051. Web: www.Italianbrclts.com or www.zed.us/1332.

NEBRASKA

Laurie Brown, Simply Charming, Omaha, NE. Tel: (402) 657-4033. E-mail: charming@cox.net. Web: www.mzcharms.com.

NEVADA

Sara Hagar. Tel: (610) 407-4663. Fax: (610) 407-4662.
E-mail: sarahagar@comcast.net. Web: www.zed.us/1838

NEW JERSEY

Robin DeRosa, Long Valley, NJ. Tel: (908) 876-3020. E-mail: Robin8265@att.net. Web: www.zed.us/RobinDeRosaCharms.

NEW YORK

Lorraine M. Sules. Tel: (914) 980-1792. E-mail: Gabbie96@aol.com. Web: www.TaviasItalianCharms.com.

NORTH CAROLINA

Debra Allison, Graham, NC. Tel: (336) 570-2699.
E-mail: deballison@earthlink.net.

OHIO

Sara Hagar. Tel: (610) 407-4663. Fax: (610) 407-4662.
E-mail: sarahagar@comcast.net. Web: www.zed.us/1838

OKLAHOMA

Maurine Holt, Team Leader, Edmund, OK. Tel: (405) 818-4352. E-mail: sales@italiancharmsz.com. Web: www.zed.us/1700.

PENNSYLVANIA

Maureen M. Putnam, Independent Consultant, York, PA. Tel: (717) 840-8623. E-mail: moputnam@blazenet.net. Web: www.zed.us/2179.

SOUTH CAROLINA

Meg Todd, Greenville, SC. Tel; (864) 254-6177. E-mail: megtodd@charter.net. Web: www.zed.us/megtodd.

TENNESSEE

Deb Webb, Private Consultant, Granite City, TN. Tel: (618) 797-7104. Fax: (618) 797-7104. E-mail: charmsomy@cs.com. Web: www.zed.us/1302.

TEXAS

Karen Westbrooks, Independent Sales Consultant, Crosby, TX. Tel: (281) 462-8226. Fax: (281) 462-8196. E-mail: kswestbr@houston.rr.com. Web: www.zed.us/1495.

UTAH

Deborah Vincent, Independent Jewelry Consultant. Tel: (707) 451-7560. E-mail: CharmedPleasures@aol.com. Web: www.zed.us/CharmedPleasures.

VIRGINIA

Shannon L. Howe, Howe Charming, Ashburn, VA. Tel: (703) 623-1040. Fax: (703) 858-5091. E-mail: showe@adelphia.net. Web: www.HoweCharming.net.

WASHINGTON

Cathy Leistikow, Independent Sales Consultant, Lynnwood, WA. Tel: (425) 238-1454. E-mail: cathyscharms@aol.com. Web: www.cathyscharms.com.

WEST VIRGINIA

Judy Hunt, Independent Consultant, Winfield, WV. Tel: (304) 755-3321. Fax: (304) 755-3321. E-mail: pcqueen@adelphia.net. Web: www.zed.us/2523.

Learn More: Direct Selling Books and Web Sites

Books

More Than a Pink Cadillac: Mary Kay, Inc.'s Nine Leadership Keys to Success, by Jim Underwood (McGraw-Hill Trade, 2002).

Direct Sales: Be Better Than Good—Be Great, by Joyce M. Ross (Pelican Publishing Company, 1991)

Your First Year in Network Marketing, by Rene Reid Yarnell and Mark Yarnell (Prima Lifestyles, 1998)

Wave 4: Network Marketing in the 21st Century, by Richard Poe (Prima Lifestyles, 1999)

The Wave 4 Way to Building Your Downline, by Richard Poe (Prima Lifestyles, 2000)

Network Marketing for Dummies, by Zig Ziglar and John P. Hayes (IDG Books, 2000)

The New Professionals: The Rise of Network Marketing as the Next Major Profession, by James W. Robinson and Charles W. King (Prima Lifestyles, 2000)

Strike It Rich in Personal Selling: Techniques for Success in Direct Sales, Multi-Level and Network Marketing, by Gini Graham Scott (iUniverse, 2000)

Marketing to Women : How to Understand, Reach, and Increase Your Share of the Largest Market Segment, by Martha Barletta (Dearborn Trade, 2002)

Web Sites

www.wahmfest.org—WAHMFest

www.directsalesinfo.com

www.mlmwoman.com

www.directsales.ws

www.dsa.org—The Direct Selling Association

Appendix
Direct Sales Companies Top Ten Lists*

Top Ten Highest Commission Companies

1. Aloette Cosmetics
2. Mary Kay Cosmetics
3. Premier Designs
4. Cookie Lee Jewelry
5. Aularale Cosmetics
6. Nouveau Cosmeceuticals
7. BeautiControl Cosmetics
8. Alabaster Candles at Home
9. Passion Parties
10. Weekenders USA

Top Ten Cheapest Starter Kits Available**

1. PartyLite Gifts
2. Enchanting Scents Designs
3. The Fuller Brush Company
4. Petra Fashions
5. Woods Potpourri

6. Sweet Berry Fields
7. Avon
8. Enchanted Potions
9. Simply Satisfying Soaps
10. FemOne

Editor's Choice: Most Intriguing Companies/Unique Products

1. The Traveling Vineyard (Wine sold through in-home wine tastings)
2. UBB's Natural Family Boutique (Attachment parenting, pregnancy, and breastfeeding products)
3. Wildtree Herbs (Unique blends of herbs, spices, infused oils, and sauces free of preservatives, MSG, fillers, and anti-caking agents.)
4. Greta's Bake at Home Cookies (Unique sole product: cookie dough!)
5. Warm Spirit (Bath and body coupled with homepathics—thrilled to see it)
6. Once Upon a Family (Beautiful photo/scrapbook albums and family history books; description doesn't do them justice)
7. My Precious Kid (Invaluable ID kits for kids)
8. The Story Teller (Felt board puppets and storyboards)
9. Patchwork & Preserves (Amish craftsmanship and quality are their theme of products)
10. Quiet Places for You (A combination of products dedicated to quieting women's hearts, homes, and minds)

*Top ten lists were compiled according to information provided by companies.

**Includes companies with free basic starter kits, but more expensive larger kits.

Direct Selling Company Quick-Comparison Chart

Company	Products	Retail Commissions	Downline Commissions	Starter Kit Cost
Affordable Luxuries	Candles	25–40%	6%	$25–$199
Alabaster Candles at Home	Candles	40–50%	10%, 5%	$295
Aloette Cosmetics	Cosmetics	51%	up to 16%	$5,000 franchise
The Angel Company	Rubber Stamps	25%	2%	$75–$300
Arbonne International	Botanical Skin Care Products	35%	4%	$29–$65
AtHome America	Home Décor	20–30%	2–12%	$149
Aularale Cosmetics	Cosmetics	up to 50%	8%	$150
Avon	Cosmetics	25–50%	5–12%	$10
Azante Jewelry	Jewelry	25%	*	$99–$500
BeautiControl Cosmetics	Cosmetics	40–50%	4–12%	$99–$250
Big Enough	Children's Clothing	10–30%	2–5%	$40–$79
The Bittersweet Candle Company	Candles	30–40%	2–10%	$70–$89

Company	Products	Retail Commissions	Downline Commissions	Starter Kit Cost
Cell Tech	Nutritional: Super Blue Green Algae®	5–25%	5–15%	$100
Charmed Moments	Charm Jewelry	30–46%	2–9%	$249–$395
Chic Pursenality	Handbags & Jewelry	25%	up to 80%	$25–$150
Close to My Heart	Rubber Stamps & Scrapbooking Supplies	22–32%	2%	$89.95
Cookie Lee Jewelry	Jewelry	50%	8%+	Varies: Consultant chooses which jewelry to buy
Country Bunny Bath and Body	Bath and Body Products	15%	5–10%	$179
Creative Memories	Scrapbooking Supplies	30–45%	3–12%	$195
DeMarle at Home	Flexipan and Housewares	20–31%	2–11%	$149.95
Discovery Toys	Educational Toys and Games	25–50%	7–15%	$149
Ecoquest	Air Quality Products		16–42%	
Enchanted Potions	Handmade Soaps, Bath & Body Products	30–40%	5%	$10
Enchanting Scents Designs	Candles	30–33%	3%	Free
FemOne	Nutritionals & Cosmetics	30%	15%, 5%	$24.95–$49.95

Company	Products	Retail Commissions	Downline Commissions	Starter Kit Cost
For Your Pleasure	Adults Toys & Intimate Novelties	up to 50%	10%	$250–$1,000
The Fuller Brush Company	Household & Home Care Products	20–46%	1–26%	Free-$39.95
Gabby Goodies	Gourmet Food & Coffee	25%	Free product	$29.95–$49.95
Gifted Expressions	Gourmet Foods & Spa Assortments	20%	2–7%	$289
Girls Night In	Women's Clothing, Home Décor, Spa Products, and Jewelry	20–50%	*	$25
The Gold Canyon Candle Company	Candles	17–40%	17%	$130
The Good Nature Company	Garden Accessories	25–30%	up to 5%	$150
Greta's Bake at Home Cookies	Cookie Dough	35%	3–6%	$135
HENN Workshops	Pottery, Baskets, Candles	25%	*	$99.99
Herbalife	Herbal Nutrition Products	25–50%	5–25%	$100
Highlights Jigsaw	Educational Toys & Games	20–34%	6–9%	$49–$149
Home and Garden Party	Home & Garden Décor	30–40%	3–10%	$150

Company	Products	Retail Commissions	Downline Commissions	Starter Kit Cost
Homemade Gourmet	Gourmet Food Mixes	10–20%	*	$99
The Homemaker's Idea Company	Home Décor	25%	2–5%	$175
HomeWare Creations	Homewares	15–20%	3%	$125
Jafra Cosmetics	Cosmetics, Bed & Bath Products	up to 50%	*	*
Joielle Fine Jewelry	Jewelry	25–40%	2.5–20%	$120
Lady Remington Jewelry	Jewelry	30–40%	*	*
Leaving Prints	Scrapbooking Supplies	up to 43%	up to 18%	$25
The Limu Company	Nutritional: Original Limu	varies	varies	$25
Longaberger	Handcrafted Baskets	25%	$200 product credit	$99–$399
Manuel.Zed	Charm Jewelry	35%	2%	$99–$2,000
Mary Kay Cosmetics	Cosmetics & Skin Care Products	50%	4–26%	$100
Melaleuca	Home Care, Skin Care, & Wellness Products	20%	7%+	$29
MemoryWorks	Scrapbooking Supplies	20%	Product credit only	$65
My Precious Kid	Child ID Kits	25–50%	5%	$30

Company	Products	Retail Commissions	Downline Commissions	Starter Kit Cost
NEST Family	Educational Religious Products for Children	*	*	$50
Northern Lights at Home	Candles	30–35%	*	$149–$249
Nouveau Cosmeceuticals	Skin wellness products	45%	2–8%	$49.95–$249
Nu Skin International	Skin Care & Cosmetics	25–33%	6–12%	$99–$398
Once Upon a Charm	Charm Jewelry	22%	2–3%	$130
Once Upon a Family	Scrapbooks, Albums & Accessories	up to 25%	2–8%	$125–$370
The Pampered Chef	Kitchen Wares & Gadgets	20%	*	$100
PartyLite Gifts	Candles & Gifts	25–32%	7%	Free
Passion Parties	Adult Toys and Sensual Products	40%	3–5%	$250–$450
Patchwork & Preserves	Amish Gourmet Foods & Home Décor	up to 40%	up to 15%	$50–$349
Petra Fashions	Lingerie	30%+	*	$1
The Picture Perfect Scrapbook Co.	Scrapbooking Supplies	20%	5%, 4%	$50
Premier Designs Jewelry	Jewelry	50%	10%	$395
Princess House	Homewares & Home Décor	*	*	*

Company	Products	Retail Commissions	Downline Commissions	Starter Kit Cost
Quiet Places for You	Books & Journals, Home Accessories, Spa Products	25%	*	$99–$199
Richmont Direct	Housewares, Jewelry & Holiday Products	30%	5%	$74.95–$99.95
SeneGence International	Cosmetics	20–50%	*	$45–$500
Sensaria	Skin & Body Care Produces	30%	5–12%	$115
Shaklee	Nutrition, Personal & Home Care Products	15%	5%	$19.95/year
Silpada Designs	Jewelry	30%	4–16%	$199–$1,500
Simply Satisfying Soaps	Soaps, Bed & Bath Products, Candles	30%	*	$21.95
Southern Living at Home	Home & Garden Décor	25%	2–8%	$199
Stampin' Up!	Rubber Stamps	20–30%	2–5%	$195–$229
The Story Teller	Story Boards for Children	20–35%	1–15%	$30–$100
Sweet Berry Fields	Gourmet Foods, Candles & Soaps	30%	4–15%	$9.99–$49.99
Taste of Gourmet	Gourmet Foods & Beverages	25–30%	1–4%	$75–$195

Company	Products	Retail Commissions	Downline Commissions	Starter Kit Cost
Taste of Home Parties	Cookbooks, Kitchen Wares, Home Accessories	25%	4%	$149
Tastefully Simple	Gourmet Food	20–36%	5%, 3%, 1%	$99–$170
Top Line Creations	Scrapbooking supplies	25–45%	5–10%	$100
The Traveling Vineyard	Wine	20%	2–5%	$250
Tupperware	Kitchen Wares	25–35%	3–5%	$63
Two Sisters Gourmet	Gourmet Foods	25–32%	3–7%	$99
Unique Baby Boutique	Childbirth, Baby & 0Parenting Products	25%	up to 15%	$99–$249
USANA Health Sciences	Nutritionals	10–20%	10–20%	$250–$1,250
Usborne Books at Home	Educational Books for Children	15–30%	1–11%	$199
Villa Beautiful	Home Décor	25%	5%	$199
VitaCorp	Nutritionals	*	*	$29
Warm Spirit	Spa & Bath Products, Homeopathics	25%	Gift certificates	$99–$399
Watkins International	Personal Care Products, Gourmet Foods, Cleaning Products	19%	*	$49.95–$399.99

Company	Products	Retail Commissions	Downline Commissions	Starter Kit Cost
Weekenders USA	Women's Clothing	40%	1–15%	0–$1,500 (consultant chooses sample clothing)
Wild Tree Herbs	Gourmet Culinary Blends, Infused Oils, Sauces & Dressings	25–40%	3–15%	$100
Woods Potpourri	Potpourri, Bed & Bath Products, Candles	25%	*	$9.99–$40
ZeBlooms	Floral Home Décor Products	25–30%	2–10%	$149.99

*Information not available at time of printing.

About the Editor

Michelle McGarry writes about home business, careers, and education. Her last book, *Train at Home to Work at Home* (ISBN: 0-595-28450-7) details 27 work-at-home careers and the distance-learning programs that teach them, and is available on Amazon.com and BarnesandNoble.com, or at your local bookstore. For more information about Michelle and her books, visit www.michellemedia.com.

If you are a representative from one of these companies and wish to be included as a contact in the next edition of *The Big Book of Direct Sales Careers*, visit www.bigbookofdirectsales.com.

Index

Books and Toys/For Kids

Cosmetics/Skin Care/Bed and Bath

Health and Nutrition

Clothing/Lingerie

Scrapbooking/Rubber Stamping

Candles

Jewelry/Charm Jewelry

Adult Toys/Sensual Products

Specialty/Combinations

0-595-32570-X

www.ingramcontent.com/pod-product-compliance
Lightning Source LLC
Chambersburg PA
CBHW030941180526
45163CB00002B/659
9780595325702